Enhancement of Degraded Shrub-Steppe Habitats with an Emphasis on Potential Applicability in Eastern Washington

Authors:

Peter Dunwiddie, Affiliate Professor, School of Environmental and Forest Sciences, University of Washington

Pam Camp, Ecological Consultant and former Bureau of Land Management Botanist

Technical Note 443
December 2013

Acknowledgments

A number of people generously provided their experiences and expertise for the preparation of this technical note. Katrina Strathmann (Yakama Nation), Dan Peterson (Washington Department of Fish and Wildlife), Courtney Smith (Natural Resources Conservation Service), Chuck Warner and David St. George (The Nature Conservancy), and Mel Asher (BFI Native Seeds) all enriched this technical note by sharing their restoration project experiences. Chris Sheridan and Molly Boyter (Bureau of Land Management) helped shape and improve the scope and content by providing input, guidance, and comments. Financial support for the preparation of this tech note was provided by the Bureau of Land Management.

Table of Contents

Table of Figures

Table of Tables

Abstract

There is considerable interest in restoring shrub-steppe habitats in Washington to enhance their suitability as sage-grouse habitat. The purpose of this technical note is to synthesize the experience of practitioners in Washington and nearby states, as well as draw upon published and unpublished literature, to provide recommendations and assistance to Bureau of Land Management (BLM) staff in developing more effective approaches for restoring shrub-steppe. This tech note focuses on the restoration of degraded, but still-extant, shrub-steppe habitats, particularly in areas with deeper soils, and how this can be accomplished in ways that are both ecologically effective and cost efficient. This tech note provides a seven-step framework for approaching shrub-steppe restoration, a state-and-transition model that describes seven shrub-steppe "starting states," and four "restored states" that characterize many of the conditions for partial or complete restoration of shrub-steppe habitats. The transitions linking these starting and restored states describe the changes sites must undergo to be restored. Lastly, the tech note describes the process for restoring shrub-steppe following the steps of the framework and relates these steps to the state-and-transition model.

1. Introduction

1.1 Emphasis and Focus of Technical Note

This technical note was prepared as partial fulfillment of a contract with the University of Washington under an award from the Bureau of Land Management (BLM). This award derives from ARRA (American Recovery and Reinvestment Act of 2009) funding to explore opportunities for enhancing sage-grouse (*Centrocercus urophasianus*) habitat restoration. Specifically, this effort was intended to draw upon the experience of practitioners, published and unpublished literature, and other sources to bring together information on the current state of understanding of shrub-steppe restoration. The purpose of this tech note is to synthesize information to provide recommendations and assistance to BLM agency staff in developing more effective approaches for restoring a variety of shrub-steppe habitats in eastern Washington.

This tech note focuses on a primary question: How can degraded shrub-steppe habitats, where the historical, native vegetation components have been significantly modified, be restored in ways that are both ecologically effective and cost efficient? Although the focus is on lands in eastern Washington, restoration experience in shrub-steppe habitats within this region is limited. Therefore, this tech note draws upon experience and literature that encompasses similar habitats across the arid Western United States. Restorationists in this area have confronted similar challenges and issues, and this tech note makes inferences, generates hypotheses, and suggests potential restoration strategies based upon their experiences in this larger region.

Much of the degradation and loss of shrub-steppe habitats throughout the American West has resulted from similar sources—most notably excessive and inappropriate livestock grazing, conversion to agriculture, and fires that have been larger and more frequent than the regimes from which these systems evolved prior to Euro-American settlement. As a result, several key questions repeatedly confront land managers seeking to restore these systems. These questions include: (1) How do we control invasive nonnative species that alter ecosystem properties and that are associated with losses in native diversity? (2) How do we establish and maintain native plants to restore biodiversity? and (3) How do we restore species that provide important compositional or structural components to the ecosystems? These are key questions in eastern Washington and, therefore, are the primary areas of emphasis of the restoration practices discussed in this tech note.

Restoration can be carried out at various scales, from small, intensively managed plots; to fields, pastures, and parcels of several hundred acres; and even across entire landscapes. Here, we focus on restoration practices that are carried out at the intermediate scale, spanning tens to several hundreds of acres. This is the scale at which most restoration in shrub-steppe ecosystems has taken place. This scale is generally more cost effective than small, high-intensity, plot-based efforts, and this scale is usually more ecologically meaningful. Often, intermediate-scale efforts convey benefits to a wide array of organisms with habitat requirements that encompass large acreages. Although the ranges of sage-grouse populations typically include tens of square miles, it is rarely possible, either from a practical or an economic perspective, to carry out restoration of such large landscapes.

Restoration has been carried out across a variety of vegetation types that occur within the shrub-steppe landscape of eastern Washington, including in shrub-steppe dominated by Wyoming big sagebrush (*Artemisia tridentata* ssp. *wyomingensis*) or threetip sagebrush (*A. tripartita*). Restoration has also been carried out across a variety of habitat types associated with shrub-steppe, including alkaline flats, lithosols, and various types of riparian vegetation. This tech note only focuses on restoration of the moderately deep/deep soil typically characterized by the aforementioned sagebrush species for several reasons, including:

(1) These species include many of the dominant vegetation types that comprise a large percentage of the shrub-steppe habitat in eastern Washington. Thus, a significant majority of shrub-steppe restoration in this region is likely to occur in these habitats.

(2) These vegetation types include some of the most significant and productive habitats used by sage-grouse. Hence, concentrating restoration efforts in these habitats is likely to make significant contributions to habitat restoration for this species.

(3) Much of the shrub-steppe restoration that has taken place across the arid West has occurred in sagebrush habitats similar to these. Therefore, lessons learned from these efforts elsewhere may be more transferable to the Wyoming big sagebrush and threetip sagebrush habitats in Washington, rather than to the more uncommon vegetation types.

(4) Restoration on shallow or rocky soils (lithosols) and in other specialized habitats can be extremely difficult due to a lack of commercially available plant materials, harsh growing conditions that increase the likelihood of failure, and substrates that often preclude the use of most mechanized equipment.

In addition to recalcitrant substrates, restoration of riparian habitats is also excluded from this tech note. There is considerable literature and relatively extensive experience directly related to restoration of riparian vegetation in many areas. Techniques tend to be fairly well developed, and this information is readily available in numerous books, agency publications, and scientific journals. Furthermore, methods generally tend to be fairly transferable among riparian systems in different regions.

Because the impetus of this tech note is derived from a desire to restore suitable habitat for sage-grouse in Washington, where necessary, additional emphasis is placed on describing restoration of particular vegetation components that have been identified as especially important to sage-grouse.

1.2 Restoration of Extant vs. Potential Shrub-Steppe

The vegetation conditions that occur on the moderately deep/deep-soil shrub-steppe habitats included in this tech note vary dramatically, depending not only on the current soils and climate, but also on the nature, extent, timing, and duration of the factors that have contributed to their degradation and that have resulted in their need for restoration. Thus, the starting conditions facing the restorationist at each site—and the restoration challenges that are posed—vary tremendously. Collectively, these conditions can be broken down into two major types that present notably different restoration challenges.

The first type—which we refer to here as *extant shrub-steppe*—includes sites where native species still comprise a significant component of the vegetation. These sites span a spectrum of conditions reflecting the intensity and extent of degradation, ranging from relatively intact assemblages of native species, to vegetation that may be largely or entirely missing significant portions of the shrubs, bunchgrasses, and/or forbs that comprise healthy shrub-steppe.

The second type—described here as *potential shrub-steppe*—includes sites where native species are essentially absent. Often, these sites have historically been plowed, resulting in the complete removal of native species from the site. Their current condition can range from barren, fallow agricultural fields, to dense infestations of invasive weeds, to assemblages of planted (often nonnative) cultivars (especially if they have been enrolled as Conservation Reserve Program lands). Because these types of sites are virtually lacking any of the native species that once defined them as shrub-steppe, the *potential* modifier underscores both their current condition and future possibilities with appropriate restoration actions.

These two types of sites—*extant and potential shrub-steppe*—include essentially all of the shrub-steppe restoration that takes place in Washington. Distinguishing between them is important, as there are many differences in how restoration is planned and implemented between types of sites that differ so extensively in their starting conditions. With *extant shrub-steppe*, restoration generally emphasizes the enhancement or recovery of some of the components of the ecosystem that have been degraded or damaged. In contrast, *potential shrub-steppe* generally requires the creation or replacement of all the vegetational components in ecosystems where all (or virtually all) native species have been extirpated and most ecosystem functionality has been altered or impaired. In this tech note, we refer to restoration of *potential shrub-steppe* as "full field" restoration to distinguish it from the more selective approaches often used in enhancement restoration. All of these approaches fall under the overarching embrace of "ecological restoration" (SER 2004).

Since the Washington Department of Fish and Wildlife (WDFW) developed a manual for restoring *potential shrub-steppe* (Benson et al. 2011), we primarily focus on the first type, emphasizing approaches for enhancing *extant shrub-steppe*. We also do not suggest and evaluate possible monitoring protocols in this tech note. We have provided input on the development of these sections in the WDFW manual, which synthesizes current knowledge and experience for these types of shrub-steppe restoration in Washington. Other excellent sources of information on developing monitoring programs that dovetail with objectives and project goals include Elzinga, Salzer, and Willoughby (1998) and Wirth and Pyke (2007).

Photo by Matt Lavin

2. Methods and Sources

Stabilization and improvement of degraded and damaged vegetation, wildlife habitats, soils, and range and croplands have been a concern of foresters, farmers, ranchers, and agency staff for many decades. However, it has only been in approximately the last 30 years that restoration ecology has begun to emerge as a serious science. As this field has matured, practitioners have developed and applied restoration principles and approaches to a variety of ecosystems. In most areas, this work has been carried out relatively informally, with land managers developing methods for improving conditions largely through trial and error. The exchange of information on effective restoration approaches and on-the-ground techniques has been facilitated by conferences, field trips, and a variety of journals. With this growth in numbers and geographic scope, agency and academic scientists have begun to add considerable experimental and scientific rigor to address key restoration questions and to improve on the primarily anecdotal nature of much information.

Several approaches were used to gather the most comprehensive and up-to-date information to assist in recommending the most effective strategies for restoring shrub-steppe in eastern Washington. We sought to identify potentially effective approaches based on demonstrated successes, failures and mistakes to be avoided, information gaps and research needs, and the relative costs of various approaches. The primary approaches we used include: (1) consulting practitioners actively engaged in restoring shrub-steppe in Washington and nearby states, (2) collecting and assessing case studies documenting restoration experience, and (3) scouring published and grey literature for relevant information.

2.1 Consulting Practitioners
An extensive list of practitioners was developed based on our own personal contacts with shrub-steppe restorationists and from references and recommendations from others (see Appendix 1). The practitioners belong to various agencies and organizations, including the BLM, Natural Resources Conservation Service, U.S. Geological Survey, U.S. Fish and Wildlife Service, WDFW, The Nature Conservancy, Yakama Nation, Chelan-Douglas Land Trust, and more. Most of these people were contacted directly by phone or email, to determine the extent of their experience and their willingness to share specific information.

2.2 Case Studies
In addition to collecting information and documenting experience with shrub-steppe restoration approaches, we were especially interested in identifying restoration case studies. We thought being able to examine the outcomes of particular strategies actually undertaken on eastern Washington sites would be especially helpful in determining the likelihood of different approaches being successful under various circumstances.

To gather this information in a format that would allow easy comparison of results, we collaborated with WDFW staff (especially Richard Tveten) to develop a form documenting and summarizing shrub-steppe restoration projects (see Appendix 2). Forms were then completed either by the managers who carried out the restoration actions or by interviewing managers and recording the relevant information. Ten case studies, all describing "full field" restoration projects, were compiled as part of a shrub-steppe restoration manual developed by WDFW staff and are included in that document (Benson et al. 2011). We gathered information from other agricultural field restoration projects to provide additional background for this tech note.

Comparisons of the various case studies confirmed our expectations that each restoration effort tended to use different methods of site preparation, seeding and weed control techniques, and intensity of effort. This lack of standardization limits generalizations regarding the effectiveness of different restoration approaches but is inevitable, given the differences among sites and available resources, the pioneering status of shrub-steppe restoration, and the lack of consensus among practitioners regarding optimal approaches. Much more on-the-ground experience among restorationists is needed before some of these obstacles can be overcome. However, the ecological mechanisms that shape these restored shrub-steppe communities are similar in many contexts and allow useful comparisons to be made among many projects.

In the course of gathering these case studies, it became clear that there are two primary impediments to learning from these experiences: (1) a lack of project documentation (including both methods and results) and (2) a failure to communicate outcomes (both successful and otherwise) to others. Many projects were vague on describing project objectives and site conditions prior to implementation; many included only sketchy documentation of treatments, seeding protocols, and followup actions; and almost none

contained any sort of quantitative assessment of restoration outcomes and project success.

This imprecision compounded the difficulties in relating actions to outcomes in particular projects and in looking for common patterns among projects to generalize results. We expect the shrub-steppe restoration manual prepared by the WDFW (Benson et al. 2011) will help to overcome some of these deficiencies by providing practitioners with specific guidance for accomplishing various important steps in the restoration process. To facilitate improving restoration practices among all land managers in eastern Washington shrub-steppe, we provided the WDFW with assistance and feedback on sections of their manual.

2.3 Literature Mining
We conducted an extensive search of relevant literature in an effort to identify all important sources of information that have been published relating to shrub-steppe restoration. However, as has already been noted, rigorous scientific studies documenting shrub-steppe restoration practices per se are few. Thus, much of this literature is somewhat tangential, only partially touching on relevant aspects (e.g., weed control, Conservation Reserve Program planting, etc.).

Since the peer-reviewed journal literature tends to be biased toward more experimental, replicated studies, we also sought out technical documents, presentations at meetings, and other sources in which somewhat more informal reports can be found. To make the information in these references most useful, we compiled notes for many of them, describing their relevance to shrub-steppe restoration, and incorporated this information, along with the citation data, into a database that allows users to search by topic, keywords, author, etc., and access abstracts, full articles, presentation images, etc. This information is available upon request from the BLM Spokane District. We have attempted to generalize the findings, results, and observations in these sources to make hypotheses about the success of various restoration techniques in Washington.

Most of this literature is primarily relevant to particular aspects of shrub-steppe restoration. The most useful are cited in this tech note. The most comprehensive publication that provides an overview of much recent, relevant literature is the volume "Greater Sage-Grouse: Ecology and Conservation of a Landscape Species and Its Habitats," edited by Knick and Connelly (2011). Several of the chapters in this book provide reviews on the conservation and restoration of shrub-steppe habitats across the West. Also, Benson et al. (2011) contains extensive information on restoring potential shrub-steppe in Washington and is directly relevant to many of the topics contained in this tech note.

Photo by Peter Dunwiddie

Photo by Peter Dunwiddie

3. Physical and Biological Characteristics of Shrub-Steppe

Detailed conditions of the physical and biological environments of a particular site being restored must be considered when restoring shrub-steppe habitats in eastern Washington. Fortunately, there are several sources of information readily available that provide much of this information to land managers. General conditions are briefly reviewed here, along with the specific sources where this information can be obtained for specific sites.

3.1 Climate

Precipitation, temperature, and growing season are key factors that will affect the choice of plant materials, the timing and mode of installing them, and the likelihood of success. Several web-based sources provide detailed estimates of these parameters. We found two to be particularly useful for obtaining site-specific climate information. Historical information for average climate parameters at individual stations can be obtained from the Western Regional Climate Center at *http://www.wrcc. dri.edu/summary/Climsmwa.html*. Estimated values for small-size grid cells can be found using the PRISM Climate Group's Data Explorer tool at *http://prismmap.nacse.org/nn/index.phtml*. Both tools provide data for all of eastern Washington.

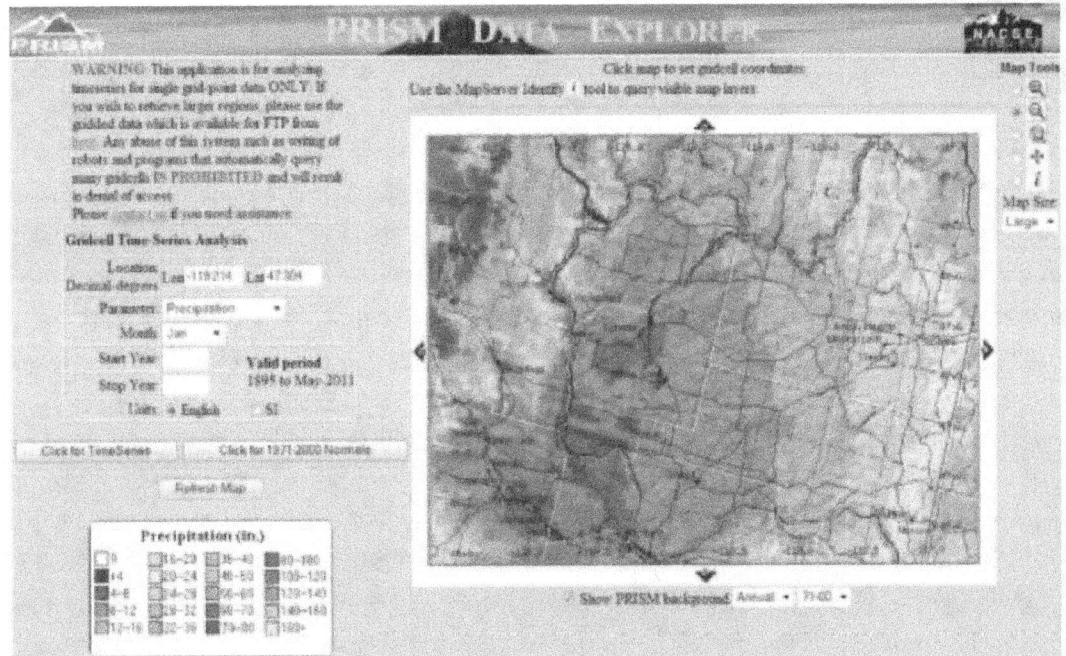

Figure 1. Average annual precipitation in eastern Washington, 1971-2000 (Source: *http://prismmap.nacse.org/nn/index.phtml*).

Figure 1 presents a screen shot of annual average precipitation from the PRISM website for the period 1971-2000 for eastern Washington. This clearly illustrates the moisture gradient across the region, with the driest conditions found in Benton County (4-8 inches), increasing to 8-12 inches in much of Grant and Douglas Counties, and 12-16 inches and higher as one moves eastward across Lincoln and Adams Counties toward Spokane. Temperatures present similar patterns, with highest maximum temperatures in Benton County and cooler conditions to the north and east.

From a restoration perspective, the variability in amount and seasonality of precipitation and extreme temperatures are critical. In the arid sites, even when site preparation has been thorough and plant materials have been carefully selected, restoration efforts can fail simply due to insufficient moisture or other adverse climatic conditions beyond a manager's control.

3.2 Topography and Geology

Shrub-steppe in Washington ranges from elevations around 400 feet in Benton County to about 3,500 feet in Douglas and Okanogon Counties. Topography varies from relatively flat alluvial bottoms to steep slopes in some canyons. Basalt bedrock underlies many sites throughout the Columbia Basin. This basalt is at or close to the surface in many areas where Missoula floods scoured off the overlying soils. Sites with deeper soils generally are derived from fine-grained loess deposits (which blanketed much of the basalt in late glacial times, but which were eroded down by Missoula floods in many areas) or from reworked loess and colluvium in canyon bottoms and floodplains where outwash and Missoula floods redeposited sediments.

3.3 Soils

The Natural Resources Conservation Service of the U.S. Department of Agriculture has created a website that provides site-specific soils information across the region. Accessed at *http://websoilsurvey.nrcs.usda.gov/ app/WebSoilSurvey.aspx*, this site is extremely useful for gathering precise information on mapped soil variations within restoration sites. Ownership boundary layers are included for most federal agency lands, although the

site currently (September 2013) does not include BLM ownership in Washington.

Soils in eastern Washington vary greatly in depth, texture, and chemistry. Sites with moderately deep to deep soils, which are the focus of this tech note, may be 2-3 feet deep (or more) and generally are loams that range in texture from silty to sandy and gravelly. Common soil series encountered in the Swanson Lakes area include Esquatzel, Ritzville, Stratford, Beckley, Benge, and Farrell, and common soil series encountered in the Moses Coulee area include Touhey, Stubblefield, Renslow, Zen, Benwy, and Alstown.

3.4 Vegetation

Descriptions of shrub-steppe vegetation in eastern Washington largely rely on the seminal work of Rex Daubenmire, which is summarized in a monograph published in 1970 (Daubenmire 1970). Although many of the species names have changed, this work still represents the primary reference for characterizing the vegetation and species occurring in these habitats. Daubenmire identified three shrub-dominated "habitat types" that characterized the arid interior of eastern Washington. These describe the primary vegetation types that historically would have dominated deeper soil sites in this region in the absence of major disturbance, such as fire or livestock grazing. Foremost among these is the Wyoming big sagebrush/bluebunch wheatgrass (*Artemisia tridentata wyomingensis/Pseudoroegneria spicata*) habitat type, the range of which closely coincides with those areas receiving less than 12 inches of average annual precipitation in Figure 1. This habitat type predominates across most of south-central Washington and is the primary focus of this tech note, along with a second big sagebrush-dominated type, Wyoming big sagebrush/Idaho fescue (*Artemisia tridentata wyomingensis/Festuca idahoensis*), which occurs in slightly moister areas to the north and east. A third shrub-dominated type, the threetip sagebrush/Idaho fescue (*A. tripartita/F. idahoensis*), occurs in some areas of west-central Lincoln and Adams Counties.

Daubenmire and others have attempted to reconstruct the historical composition of these communities by examining relatively pristine relics (Daubenmire 1970). These and similar sites comprise the baseline reference points for what healthy, intact shrub-steppe should look like. Conclusions about species abundance and composition in restored and sustainably managed shrub-steppe are derived from detailed analyses of these areas. The Natural Resources Conservation Service has used similar information to develop ecological site descriptions for many areas of eastern Washington, based on soil, aspect, and climatic characteristics of individual sites. These descriptions can be accessed via *http://websoilsurvey.nrcs.usda.gov/app/WebSoilSurvey.aspx* or through Natural Resources Conservation Service Field Office Technical Guides at *http://efotg.sc.egov.usda. gov/treemenuFS.aspx*. From the Field Office Technical Guide website, select the county, click on "Section II" in the dropdown menu on the left, and then select the "Ecological Site Descriptions" folder. These websites present lists of commonly encountered native species, which can be useful in determining potential species to restore. Since the percent composition of these ecological site descriptions is based on forage production rather than an ecological measure such as canopy cover, they do not equate directly with desired seed mix specifications. However, they do provide a general indication of both species dominance and diversity. The descriptions also often lack many forbs that may have been locally important (often forbs are only listed to genus); thus, ecological site descriptions may need to be augmented from other sources to provide comprehensive species information for restoration purposes.

The composition and structure of these habitat types vary considerably between sites and within a site over time (see Section 5). Daubenmire (1970) described these types in a relatively undisturbed state, where succession has been allowed to progress for many decades. Big sagebrush cover generally ranges from 5-20% in most stands. Where threetip sagebrush is dominant, cover values are similar. Cover of dominant bunchgrass may be 40-60% or higher, especially in moister sites. In addition to *Pseudoroegneria spicata*, commonly associated bunchgrasses in the Wyoming big sagebrush habitat types can include *Hesperostipa comata* (=*Stipa comata*), *Achnatherum thurberianum* (=*Stipa thurberiana*), *Poa cusickii*, and *Elymus elymoides* (=*Sitanion hystrix*). *Poa secunda* is a smaller statured bunchgrass that also commonly occurs. *F. idahoensis* is dominant in the threetip sagebrush habitat types, along with *P. spicata, P. secunda*, and others. Forbs tend to be more diverse and abundant in moister sites.

Nonindigenous species are present in virtually all shrub-steppe communities. Whether they have been deliberately introduced for their economic value; accidentally brought in; or dispersed by wind, water, or animals from a distant source, nonnative species are widespread. Many, if not most, are of little concern from a restoration perspective, having little impact on the native plants and animals. However, a small number of nonnative species have competitive and dispersal abilities that enable them to reproduce abundantly, compete aggressively with native species, and distribute themselves widely across the landscape. They may negatively impact native species through direct competition for water or nutrients, allelopathic influences, or by altering ecological processes in ways that are deleterious to natives. Cheatgrass is a prime example. It outcompetes seedlings of many native species by germinating and growing rapidly in the early fall, and dense infestations of adult plants provide continuous, highly flammable fuels that may result in large, more frequent, and less patchy burns than occurred historically (McIver et al. 2010). In addition to such nonnatives that are generally considered "weeds," other nonindigenous species that are frequently planted for forage, habitat, or soil stabilization purposes may also pose similar threats to native biodiversity due to their strong competitive abilities.

3.5 Ecological Dynamics

Shrub-steppe vegetation types in Washington did not evolve under heavy grazing pressure from bison and other large ungulates (Daubenmire 1970; Mack and Thompson 1982). Hence, the dominant bunchgrasses and forbs of these ecosystems are not resilient to most current livestock grazing regimes. Where sites have experienced heavy grazing, native bunchgrasses and forbs are reduced or absent, and introduced annual grasses such as *Bromus tectorum, Poa bulbosa,* and *Taeniatherum caput-medusae,* which are more tolerant of this pressure, may be abundant. Big sagebrush may be reduced due to mechanical breakage; alternatively, sagebrush can become overly dense and tall in overgrazed sites.

These communities also have not evolved under regimes with frequent fire (Daubenmire 1970). Recent studies suggest that fire return intervals historically may have been on the order of 50-120 years (Baker 2006) or perhaps as long as 200-350 years (Mensing, Livingston, and Barker 2006; Baker 2011). Big sagebrush will not resprout after fire and may be completely removed from ecosystems if frequent large fires prevent recolonization by the eradication of all nearby seed sources. In contrast, most other shrubs in these habitat types, including *Artemisia tripartita, Chrysothamnus viscidiflorus, Ericameria nauseosa, Tetradymia canescens,* and *Grayia spinosa,* generally resprout after fire and may increase in abundance in the absence of big sagebrush.

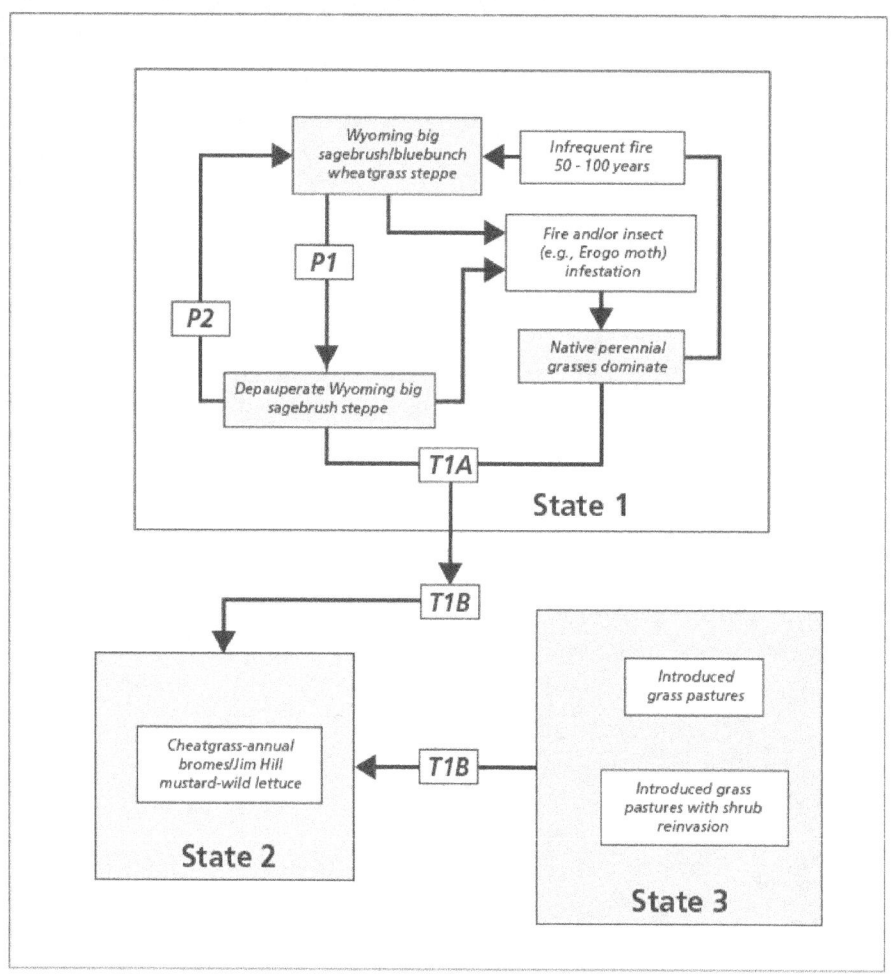

Figure 2. Basic state-and-transition model for Wyoming big sagebrush/bluebunch wheatgrass steppe. Large boxes surrounding each state represent ecological thresholds. P1 = grazing at inappropriate intensities or seasons; P2 = appropriate grazing practices; T1A and T1B = P1 + drought, fire, etc. (Source: http://efotg.sc.egov.usda.gov/treemenuFS.aspx).

The dynamics of shrub-steppe ecosystems have been debated by rangeland ecologists for years. Various paradigms have advanced, two of the main being the range model and the state-and-transition model (STM). The range model basically describes the dynamics of these ecosystems as continuous and reversible, whereas the STM recognizes more discontinuous and nonreversible ecosystems (Briske, Fuhlendorf, and Smeins 2003). STMs are generally more widely embraced by ecologists today, and these models are considered to be more useful in approaching restoration questions and strategies.

An example of a generalized STM developed by the Natural Resources Conservation Service for Wyoming big sagebrush-dominated shrub-steppe is shown in Figure 2, which depicts the role of fire and grazing in this ecosystem. Basic points of this model include: (1) frequent fire can remove the sagebrush shrubs from the ecosystem; (2) excessive or inappropriately timed grazing can result in the degradation of these communities, with a corresponding loss of native species and spread of invasive annuals; and (3) when such practices are prolonged, severe, or combined with drought or fire, the vegetation can be pushed across a threshold into another state altogether, dominated almost entirely by weedy annuals. Recovering back across this threshold from such conditions generally cannot occur without considerable restoration efforts (i.e., succession, or passive restoration, will not return ecosystems in these states to their historical, predisturbance state).

More sophisticated STMs for this ecosystem have been developed by Laycock (1991); Hemstrom et al. (2002); Briske, Fuhlendorf, and Smeins (2005); Briske et al. (2008); Bestelmeyer (2006); Bestelmeyer et al. (2009); McIver et al. (2010); and Davies and Sheley (2011). In Section 5, we present a modification of these STMs that considers shrub-steppe habitat types from a restoration perspective.

3.6 Sage-Grouse Habitat Requirements

Greater sage-grouse (*Centrocercus urophasianus*), and in Washington the subspecies western sage-grouse (*Centrocercus urophasianus phaios*), have been the subject of numerous studies across the Western United States. This section of the tech note draws heavily on a recent synthesis of all of this research (Knick and Connelly 2011), as well as a summary focused exclusively on the subspecies in Washington (Hays, Tirhi, and Stinson 1998).

Sage-grouse are strongly dependent on sagebrush, particularly Wyoming big sagebrush (*Artemisia tridentata* ssp. *wyomingensis*), and on sagebrush-dominated shrub-steppe for food and cover throughout much of the year (Hays, Tirhi, and Stinson 1998; Connelly, Rinkes, and Braun 2011). The bird is a wide-ranging species that uses various types of shrub-steppe habitats across the landscape during different times of its life cycle. Key shrub-steppe habitat components that are especially important to note from a restoration perspective include the following (summarized from Hays, Tirhi, and Stinson (1998) and Connelly, Rinkes, and Braun (2011)):

Breeding habitat:
- Leks (i.e., an area where birds gather to attract mates during the breeding season) occur in relatively open ground, with less herbaceous and shrub cover than surrounding areas.
- Most nests are under large bushes (40-80 cm), in areas with 15-25% canopy cover.
- Extensive (50%) cover and tall grass (greater than 15 cm) provides important cover for nests.
- Insects are important food for early brood rearing.
- Brood success is greater in areas with extensive forbs and herbaceous vegetation.
- Close proximity to shrubs and taller herbaceous vegetation is important for protective cover.

Summer and late brood-rearing habitat:

- Forbs become important food for late brood rearing.
- Water developments are not typically used by sage-grouse and tend to attract predators.

Autumn and winter habitat:

- Sagebrush becomes the dominant food source.
- The birds rely almost exclusively on sagebrush exposed above snow (greater than 25 cm and greater than 15% canopy cover) for forage and shelter.
- Taller sagebrush is especially important during deep snows.
- Wintering sites typically face south or west.

Based on the habitat components, the following are key shrub-steppe management implications (summarized from Connelly, Rinkes, and Braun (2011) and Aldridge et al. (2008)):

- Some agricultural areas may provide habitat in the summer, but large blocks of sagebrush are critical for reproduction and overwintering.
- Restoring herbaceous species is important, but impacts to sagebrush (wintering habitat) should be minimized or avoided.
- Maintain large expanses of sagebrush habitat, and enhance the quality and connectivity of those patches.
- Maintaining natural variation in cover and height of shrub overstory and herbaceous understory is important. Shrub-steppe should not be managed for a single value or narrow range.

Photo by Derek Oyen

4. General Approaches to Shrub-Steppe Restoration

Both the theory and practice of ecological restoration, including in shrub-steppe ecosystems, have progressed significantly in the last several decades. Increasingly, practitioners are veering away from simply removing undesirable species (generally, invasive weeds and species of low-forage or wildlife value) and establishing desirable ones (often native and high-value species). Instead, practitioners are more often using approaches that place species composition and community structure in a much more dynamic and process-oriented context. Today, the focus of the most successful restoration efforts usually is on establishing successional trajectories that will, over time, return the ecosystem toward a healthier, more sustainable state that is both resilient (e.g., able to recover quickly following disturbance) and resistant to change following many disturbances. Greater efforts are made to remove processes that contributed to the damage or degradation of the ecosystem (e.g., excessive grazing, too frequent fire, sources of invasive species) and to ensure that critical ecological components (e.g., keystone species, appropriate soil conditions, sources of native seed, etc.) are in place and sustainable (SER 2004).

An important aspect of the restoration process is the selection of restoration species. Generally, success is most likely when the species selected for inclusion (often based on comparisons with reference sites) are well-adapted to the environmental conditions—including the disturbance regime—of the site being restored. Today, for most shrub-steppe restoration, it is widely recommended that a diverse assemblage of compatible native species be used whenever possible. For example, Sheley et al. (2008) strongly recommend using local native species wherever possible, noting that natives are more likely to promote ecological stability and community integrity and to reduce the risk of introducing aggressive or invasive species. This is a significant departure from many past range management practices that are still widely followed today in the rehabilitation of degraded grazing lands and in the revegetation of burned landscapes. These practices use an average of 4-5 nonnative species and focus on only a few restoration objectives, such as stabilizing soil, providing livestock forage, or suppressing weeds (Pyke 2011). Often overlooked are the broad array of ecological benefits and synergistic interactions produced by complex ecosystems that include a full complement of native plant species.

Deciding whether to undertake such site rehabilitation, rather than to restore native shrub-steppe with a diverse assemblage of native species that embrace a variety of life forms and occupy numerous ecological niches, can be difficult. Rehabilitation is often simpler, the seeds may be more readily available and less costly, and the nonnative species may have more predictable germination characteristics and competitive abilities than native species, all of which may add to the appeal of this approach. Ultimately, the decision about which approach is appropriate on a site needs to be guided by a clear articulation of the restoration objectives. For many of the habitats used by sage-grouse in Washington, the preponderance of current research strongly points toward restoration of shrub-steppe comprised of tall native bunchgrasses, diverse native forbs, and big sagebrush (Hays,

Tirhi, and Stinson 1998; Connelly, Rinkes, and Braun 2011). However, in some highly degraded ecosystems, and when resources are unavailable to sustain comprehensive restoration efforts, rehabilitation of key habitat components may be the only viable option (Pyke 2011).

The more refined approaches advocated by many experts today are based on the recognition that single entry, one-shot restoration attempts rarely succeed. "Quick fixes" and rehabilitation efforts that address one or two problems often offer short-term outcomes that may be superficially promising but offer few of the long-term benefits of restored natural ecosystems. Rather, managers, as well as scientists, are recognizing that restoring historical successional trajectories in shrub-steppe ecosystems generally is an ongoing process, requiring multiple entries and continuing management to restart successional processes and reestablish key ecosystem components (Cox and Anderson 2004; Krueger-Mangold, Sheley, and Svejcar 2006; Sheley et al. 2008). These and other authors have used "successional management" and "assisted succession" to describe these approaches.

Successional management incorporates concepts of ecological theory to reduce the cost, increase the ecological benefits, and enhance the likelihood of success of shrub-steppe restoration. For example, integrating a recognition of the importance of ecological niches, seed availability, and seed dispersal, together with an understanding of how different disturbances can affect all of these factors, can help guide the development of restoration strategies that can favor the establishment of native species over nonnatives.

Shrub-steppe restoration that follows successional management principles generally incorporates an understanding of ecosystem dynamics that is based on state-and-transition (Westoby, Walker, and Noy-Meir 1989) or ball-and-cup (Laycock 1991) ecological models. This approach is critical, as it helps land managers identify irreversible transitions and alternate stable states that typify their sites and helps clarify the magnitude and duration of effort likely to be required to restore a site. Thus, if an ecological threshold has been crossed, significant resource investments (rather than moderate tweaking) will be required to restart or redirect succession on a desired trajectory. For example, instead of merely resting a site from grazing for a few years, managers may need to make multiple herbicide applications to control weeds, and they may need to seed a diversity of natives to establish species that have been extirpated from a site. In Sections 5 and 6, where we explore potential strategies for restoring degraded shrub-steppe, we approach restoration from the perspective of current and desired ecological states and the nature of the transitions needed to move the ecosystem between these states.

Regardless of the particular strategies employed, successful restoration efforts generally follow a systematic sequence of steps in approaching the overall task of restoring the composition and function of the ecosystem. These approaches differ somewhat in style, sequence, detail, and emphasis. Two documents are particularly worth mentioning here, as they contrast considerably in all of these areas, Clewell, Rieger, and Munro (2005) and Sheley et al. (2008). We found both to be useful and instructive in approaching shrub-steppe restoration in Washington and have developed the restoration process described in this tech note using guidance from both documents.

The "Guidelines for Developing and Managing Ecological Restoration Projects" (Clewell, Rieger, and Munro 2005) outlines an approach to ecological restoration that is designed to be applicable to a wide array of sites and types of projects. The 51 steps presented in this document anticipate most scenarios that typically arise, and the steps are comprehensive enough that key steps are not overlooked. The steps are grouped into six major sections: (1) conceptual planning, (2) preliminary tasks, (3) implementation planning, (4) project implementation, (5) post-implementation tasks, and (6) evaluation and publicity. In contrast, a recent U.S. Forest Service publication (Sheley et al. 2008) provides an explicit guide for restoring shrub-steppe ecosystems. Although its emphasis is on sites in the Great Basin that have been degraded by invasive weeds, the approach and details are directly applicable to the types of shrub-steppe restoration in the Columbia Basin covered in this tech note. Figure 3 summarizes all the steps in this document in the form of a modified decision tree.

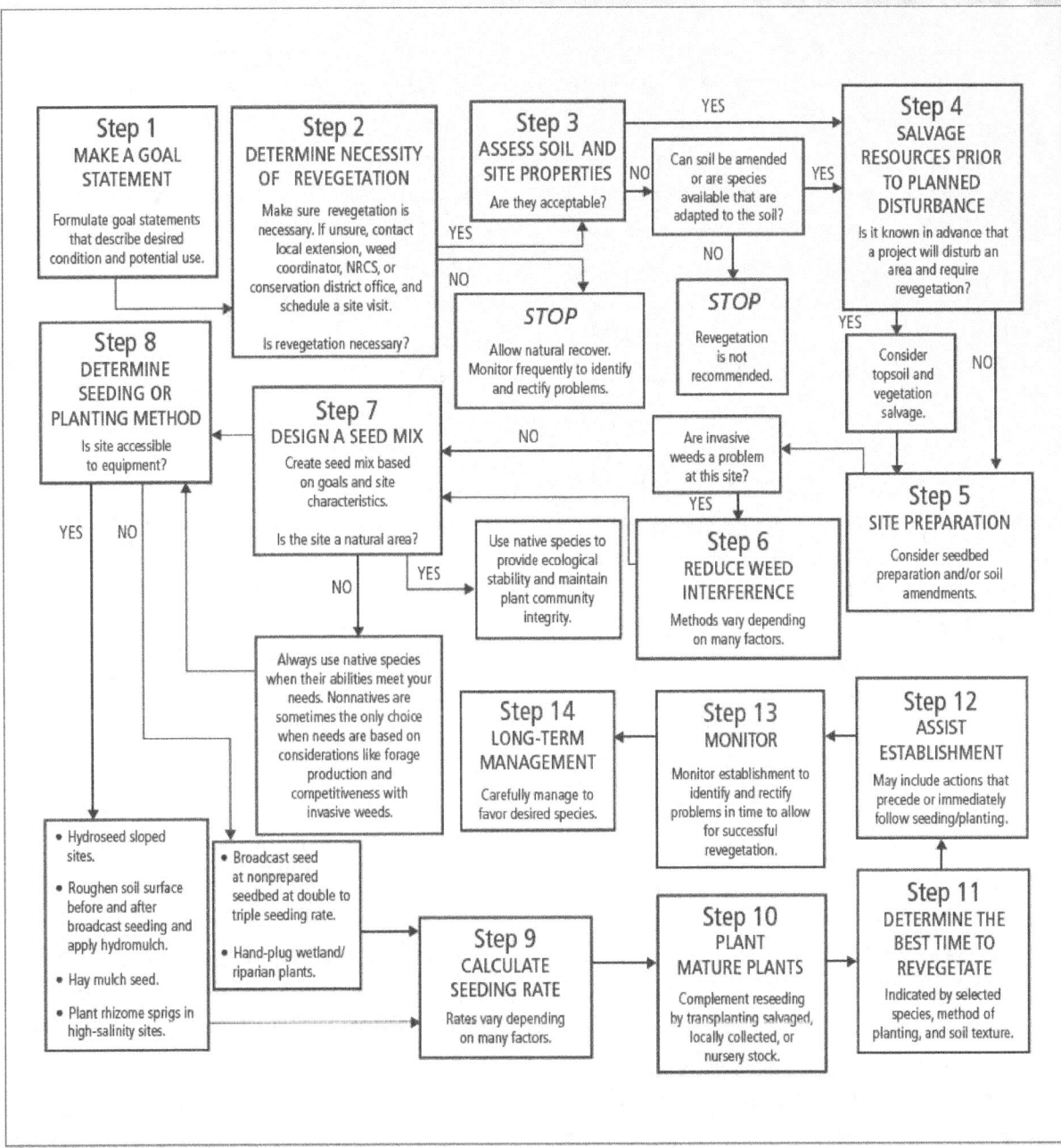

Figure 3. Example of a sequential approach for restoring shrub-steppe habitats (Source: Sheley et al. (2008) - Figure 1).

In this tech note, we have drawn on and synthesized material from both of these sources, as well as several other restoration guides, to present a sequence of steps that include considerations and strategies for restoring shrub-steppe. These steps are expanded upon in Section 6 and are illustrated using an example in Appendix 3. The main components of this approach include:

(1) **Set restoration goals.** Goal statements describe what restoration actions are intended to accomplish. It is worthwhile to revisit goals occasionally to determine if they remain realistic, based on information and experience acquired as the project progresses. Goals are more general and overarching than objectives, which usually are developed later in the restoration process once more site-specific information has been gathered (see step 3). Examples of restoration goals might include: "restore a healthy native shrub-steppe community" or "restore healthy sage-grouse habitat."

(2) **Assess the site.** This step includes gathering information about the physical and biological conditions on the site, mapping how these conditions vary across the site, documenting site histories where possible, noting relevant information regarding adjoining properties, and describing the overall landscape context. This information is then used to characterize the starting state and identify the key factors that are likely to influence restoration outcomes (e.g., stresses, site constraints, etc.).

(3) **Define spatially and temporally explicit restoration objectives.** Setting objectives is one of the most important steps in restoration planning. Objectives provide an explicit link between restoration goals (step 1) and on-the-ground actions (step 7). In developing objectives, one needs to consider the various possible alternative end points for restoration, as well as the feasibility of reaching them. It can be useful to examine

various reference sites and use ecological models (such as the Vegetation Dynamics Development Tool/Path Landscape Model and STMs) to identify and choose from several possible restoration end points. Ecological models may also assist in assessing the feasibility of different restoration scenarios by identifying transition pathways and highlighting where ecological thresholds may exist that could impede success.

To be realistic and achievable, both site characteristics (step 2) and project constraints (step 6) should be considered when defining objectives. Thus, it is necessary to revisit and, if necessary, revise objectives as the project is developed. It is particularly important to ensure that restoration objectives are both spatially and temporally explicit. Portions of a site may differ significantly from one another, and objectives need to reflect this spatial variability. Thus, some objectives may apply only to a portion of a site. Similarly, objectives for year 1 of a project will often be quite different than what they will be in years 3, 5, or 10. If only the final desired project outcome is clearly stated (e.g., year 20), it may be difficult or impossible to assess intermediate progress and make the necessary adaptive management interventions to successfully guide successional trajectories.

Objectives should also include performance measures. These are essential for evaluating progress toward meeting short-, medium-, and long-term project objectives, since these measures form the basis around which an effective monitoring program can be developed (step 5). Once objectives have been defined, it is advisable to revisit restoration goals (step 1) to see if they still are reasonable.

(4) **Identify needed alterations.** Once objectives are articulated, start and end states are identified, and ecological transitions that are necessary to

move a site from its current state are identified, one can proceed to describe the changes in physical and biotic conditions that will be needed to move the site toward the restoration goal. This should not be confused with step 5, which describes how these changes can be accomplished.

(5) **Assess project constraints.** In addition to site characteristics assessed in step 2, other logistical factors and project management considerations can affect project outcomes and need to be carefully assessed. It is important to ensure necessary resources, such as sufficient money, manpower, specific equipment, and native seed of the species and quantities required, will be available at the time they are needed. Future uses of the restored site, such as livestock grazing or recreational use, must be considered. Factors that may impose constraints on the timing or duration of restoration activities must be recognized, such as seasonality of precipitation, when funds must be obligated or spent, etc.

(6) **Identify treatments and develop monitoring programs.** This step identifies the actual restoration strategies that will be used to bring about the ecological transitions—preparing the site, reducing weeds, establishing natives, and accomplishing any of the other restoration objectives. It is useful to develop monitoring protocols at this time as well, for several reasons. Monitoring protocols can be clearly linked to restoration objectives, designed with time and manpower limitations firmly in mind, and developed to provide important and timely feedback for adapting and revising restoration actions, depending on the treatment results.

(7) **Apply treatments and monitor effectiveness.** It is important to approach each treatment or

manipulation of a site as a learning opportunity. Successful restoration rarely occurs with a single entry at a site. Usually, it is an iterative process, in which multiple treatments are applied over time. Important steps in this treatment sequence are planned in step 4, but often, responses may not result entirely as expected. For example, weeds may not be controlled as anticipated, or planted species may fail to establish. In such cases, it is important for managers to detect these unexpected outcomes in a timely manner and to try to understand why they may have occurred, so that they can take effective actions to correct them.

This is the essence of adaptive management (e.g., see Reever Morghan, Sheley, and Svejcar (2006)), and to be successfully applied to ecological restoration, two features are particularly important. First, site manipulations should be regarded as experiments wherever possible. This means basing them on hypotheses about ecological properties, functions, and responses; applying treatments consistently, with replications and controls as appropriate and feasible; and reliably documenting actions. And second, a carefully designed monitoring program must be consistently employed. When carried out thoughtfully and efficiently, monitoring can result in enormous cost savings by preventing problems from mushrooming out of control before they are detected, and monitoring may even prevent entire project failures. Using information on well-documented treatments and careful observation of results, managers can "close the loop" on adaptive management by understanding the successes and shortcomings of initial restoration efforts, deciding whether subsequent manipulations are necessary, designing followup treatments that use lessons learned, and basing these actions on current information from the restoration site.

5. A Restoration State-and-Transition Model for Shrub-Steppe

In Figure 4, we have taken the concepts underlying traditional STMs for shrub-steppe vegetation types and applied them specifically to the sage-grouse habitat restoration context of this tech note.

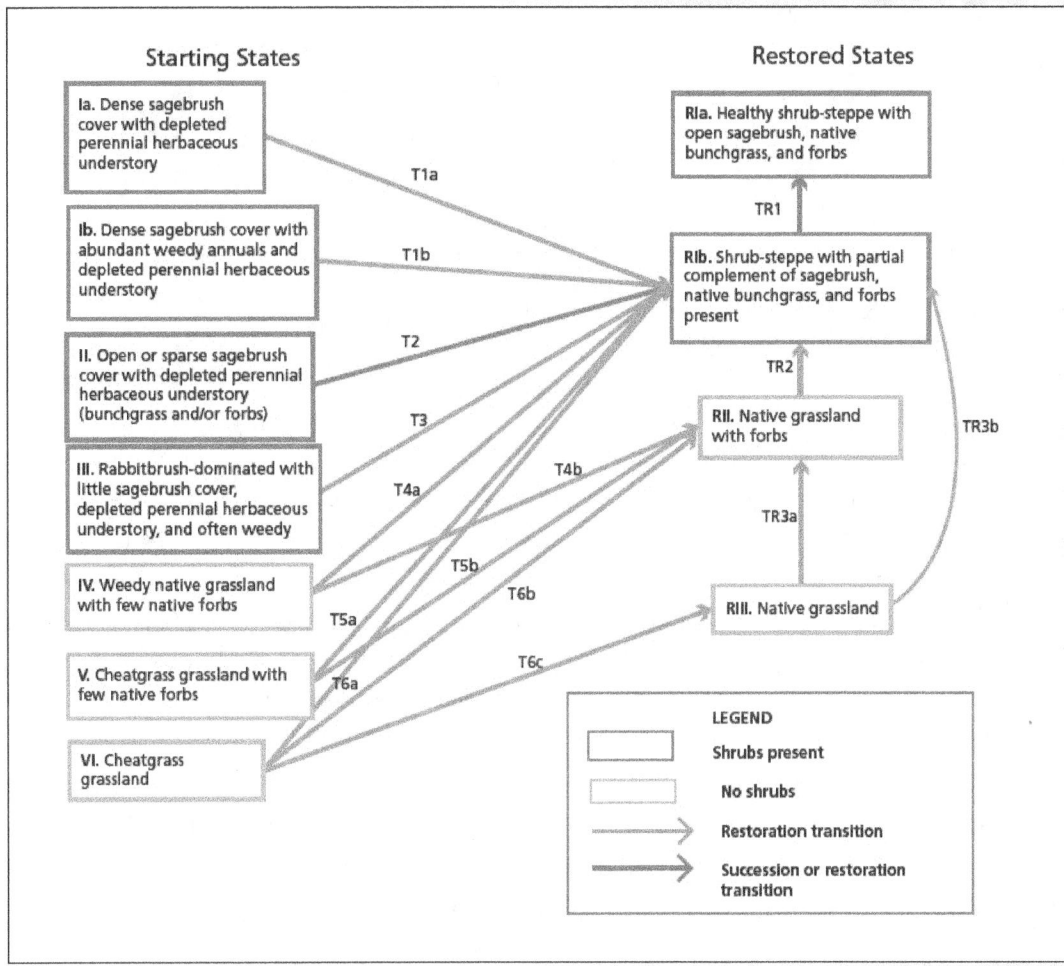

Figure 4. State-and-transition model for shrub-steppe in Washington, illustrating key vegetation states of importance to restoration managers. The model primarily applies to shrub-steppe with deeper soils and moderate moisture, capable of supporting big sagebrush communities. Transitions (T) describe the changes in composition brought about by management actions that are designed to restore components of the desired vegetative condition. This model does not explicitly include full field restoration, although this may be an appropriate alternative in some cases with States IV-VI. "Starting State" is the degraded, nondesired site for which restoration is contemplated. Transitions with red arrows may occur through natural succession and not require active restoration. See text for additional details.

This model is based on our experience with different types of degraded shrub-steppe commonly encountered in Washington and on the restoration challenges these different types present. It differs from traditional ecological models in several important respects:

(1) The various starting states emphasize differences in vegetation composition and structure that are not usually all distinguished as distinct states in traditional models. These more detailed differences often are of considerable importance from a restoration perspective, in which specific knowledge about such characteristics help define restoration strategies. These differences are generally omitted from traditional models in which depicting such detail would be overly confusing and would add little to the ecological understanding of the ecosystem.

(2) Different managers will have somewhat different restoration goals, depending on budgets, feasibility, agency priorities, etc. Thus, restoration end points ("Restored States" in Figure 4) also may differ in compositional details that are important from a restoration perspective. However, the restored states might not represent differences that typically result from the operation of key ecological processes, as depicted in traditional models.

(3) The transitions that depict movement of vegetation from a starting state to a restored state in this model represent the changes that would be expected to occur as a result of effective restoration actions. For the sake of clarity, we have not included many of the transitions that usually are depicted in models and that relate to typical ecological processes such as grazing, fire, etc.

(4) STMs generally describe different states that tend to be relatively stable, although they may have multiple "phases" (as shown in Figure 2) within a single state, among which an ecosystem

may move without changing state. Transitions (following disturbance pathways) describe the movement of an ecosystem from one phase to another (within a state), or across an ecological threshold from one stable state to another. The former may occur with little or no expenditure of outside effort and can result from normal ecological disturbances or succession. On the other hand, transitions that cross ecological thresholds tend to be irreversible without extensive restoration effort.

In Figure 4, most of the boxes depict states separated by transitions that we believe are, indeed, generally irreversible without restoration, and the transitions linking most of these states (green arrows) come about through management actions. However, in some instances, some of the states we have identified may be more accurately described as phases within a single state. In such cases, succession, if given enough time, may return an ecosystem to a different condition (phase, rather than state). But under a restoration scenario, land managers may choose to hasten this successional process (which may take decades) through restoration actions. We have identified such transitions with red arrows, indicating where restoration may not be necessary and where passive restoration (allowing succession to proceed) may be an alternative.

5.1 Restoration State-and-Transition Model Description

Degraded shrub-steppe typically has been modified from its presumed original condition (variously described as its historical state, pristine state, or reference condition) in several ways. Usually, the composition and/or abundance of native species have been altered to a condition outside their historical natural range of variability. Ecological processes, such as fire frequency and extent, may have been similarly altered as well. Furthermore, invasive nonnative plants may have become established and may have altered soil conditions, fire regimes, and the competitive balance among species. Frequently, these types of changes involve entire functional groups of species, such as native perennial forbs, bunchgrasses, and dominant shrubs.

The starting states included in Figure 4 (Roman numerals I-VI) describe many of the conditions of altered species composition and structure typically encountered in degraded shrub-steppe. Restored states (RI-RIII) characterize the general composition and structure of shrub-steppe ecosystems in which at least some groups of native species have been returned to a historical condition. There should be considerable concordance between the description of the restored state (see Section 5.3) and the goal set for a restoration project (see Section 4). Transitions (T1-T6 and TR1-TR3) describe the changes between these states that restoration actions are intended to accomplish. The range of actual restoration actions that we hypothesize will most successfully effect these transitions are described in Section 6.7.

It is important to recognize that there is considerable variation in shrub-steppe composition, structure, and condition that may, at times, be difficult to fit within the states defined in Figure 4. Some of these variants have important implications for restoration feasibility, methods, or outcomes. For the sake of clarity, we have had to simplify this into a discrete number of states and transitions. However, two components that can add important variation to all of the states depicted in the model are particularly worth noting:

(1) Presence of a biological soil crust: Intact soil crusts are thought to be critical in limiting weed establishment and spread, limiting wind and water erosion of soils, and fixing soil nitrogen (Evans and Belnap 1999; Belnap and Lange 2001; Belnap et al. 2001). Although the condition of soil crusts is not depicted as a feature distinguishing different phases or states in most shrub-steppe STMs, the absence of a crust

may create a very real but often unrecognized restoration barrier or transition threshold. Since diversified crusts often take many decades or even centuries to develop and are difficult to restore, the presence and condition of biological soil crusts may be important to note when making restoration decisions (see Section 6.2).

(2) In many sites, some nonnative species that are not regarded as weeds may be important to consider when deciding restoration strategies. In Washington, many nonnative cultivars and species of wheatgrass (*Agropyron sensu lato*) have been planted in, or have found their way into, native shrub-steppe, and thus may be important constituents of the starting state. In other cases, due to considerations of cost, availability, palatability, and performance (see Section 4), some of these taxa may be considered by land managers for inclusion in restoration mixes. If land managers choose to retain them where they already exist in the starting state, or include them as part of restoration (rehabilitation) strategies because of their desirable characteristics, these taxa can significantly influence decisions regarding choices of restoration strategies and outcomes (Section 6).

5.2 Catalogue of State-and-Transition Model Starting States

This section describes the starting states (Roman numerals I-VI) in Figure 4 in greater detail.

Ia: This state consists of shrub-steppe in which the dominant shrub is denser than normal. In Wyoming big sagebrush habitat types, cover is generally in the range of 5-25%. Overgrazing of livestock is the most common factor that leads to the development of this state. Usually, the native herbaceous understory—including both forbs and bunchgrasses—has been significantly depleted. In extreme cases, there may be virtually no plants at all in the understory. This state seems to be most typical of the big sagebrush habitat types and not of the threetip sagebrush communities.

Ib: This state is similar to Ia, but cheatgrass or other weedy annuals are common or extremely abundant in the understory.

II: This shrub-dominated starting state differs from I in that sagebrush (big or threetip) cover generally occurs within its natural range of variability (approximately 5-30%). However, the understory has been degraded through the loss of native forbs and bunchgrasses. In most cases, the native understory has been largely replaced by cheatgrass or other weedy annuals (more resembling Ib than Ia). Weeds with longer life cycles, such as various knapweeds, may have become established as well.

III: This state is similar to II but dominated by rabbitbrush or shrubs other than sagebrush, which is largely or entirely absent. Sagebrush is usually removed by fire, whereas rabbitbrush species resprout and seed well after fire. These shrubs may be structurally similar to big sagebrush, but they do not provide the critical forage for sage-grouse and, therefore, are of considerably less value for sage-grouse habitat restoration. Often, past disturbance has depleted the perennial forbs and has provided an entree for weeds such as cheatgrass to establish.

IV: In states IV-VI, the sagebrush is largely absent usually due to frequent fires, although occasionally it may have been removed to promote grazing by chaining or other means. In state IV, native bunchgrasses still comprise an important part of the herbaceous vegetation. However, native forbs have been depleted, and invasive weeds (annuals and/or perennials) may be extensive.

V: This state is similar to state IV, but the native bunchgrasses are largely absent, usually due to overgrazing or very hot fires. Cheatgrass, bulbous bluegrass, ventenata (*Ventenata dubia*), tumblemustard,

and other annual weeds are often dominant. Some native forbs may persist.

VI: This is an extreme state of vegetation degradation in which very few native species of any sort persist, and the site consists almost entirely of invasive weeds, such as those listed in state V.

5.3 Catalogue of State-and-Transition Model Restored States

This section describes the restored states (RI-RIII) in Figure 4 in greater detail.

RIa: This is the reference condition or presumed historical state, with a full complement of native shrubs, grasses, and forbs occurring in abundances that are appropriate for the site and are within the natural range of variability. Biotic crusts are generally diverse and well-developed. Invasive weeds are infrequent. Site heterogeneity and natural variability in key ecological processes results in a mosaic of early-, mid-, and late-successional species and vegetation structure across the site.

RIb: This state includes representatives of all key functional groups (many shrubs, forbs, and bunchgrasses). However, some of these groups may be over or underrepresented, or the state may be deficient in some species that would have been expected historically. Either condition results in sites outside their natural range of variability in at least some of their components. A frequently encountered example is a shrub-steppe ecosystem with abundant *Poa secunda* but only sparse occurrences of larger native bunchgrasses. Often, only a portion of the expected forb component is present; some of the omissions may be late-successional species that only become established in sites that have been in a stable, healthy condition for many decades. Others may be expected to become established or spread more abundantly across a site as a result of natural dispersal. Invasive weeds are often present, but at levels that do not affect habitat function or native species abundance or are controllable with minimal effort.

RII: Variants of this state are dominated by native grasses and forbs, but the shrub component may be largely or entirely missing. Habitats that have been restored to this state usually have not had shrubs included in the restoration mix, often with the expectation that they will invade on their own. In some cases, fire may have removed stands of sagebrush, leaving the shrub component of the vegetation deficient or absent.

RIII: Native bunchgrasses dominate the vegetation, but forbs and shrubs are largely missing. These habitats usually result from restoration efforts that have included grass-heavy seed mixes, with little or no inclusion of forbs or shrubs.

5.4 Catalogue of Transitions

The following descriptions highlight the changes in the vegetative structural components (species or functional groups) that restoration actions are intended to accomplish in moving the communities from their starting states to the restored states. In most of the transitions, these changes primarily involve reducing weed abundance; enhancing the abundance and diversity of native forbs, bunchgrasses, and shrubs; and in some cases controlling shrubs (summarized in Table 1).

The *mechanisms* (restoration treatments – green lines in Figure 4) that we hypothesize can bring about these transitions are described in Sections 6.7.6 and 6.7.8. Traditional STMs typically only describe these transition mechanisms (e.g., frequent fire, heavy grazing, etc.). However, in ecological restoration, in many cases, it may not be entirely clear which are the best treatments to bring about a desired change. Therefore, it is critical to understand what needs to be changed (components) so that managers can develop and implement the most promising restoration treatments (mechanisms) and monitor both treatment success and achievement of objectives.

Although each transition is represented by a single line connecting the two states, these should not be interpreted as representing a single intervention or manipulation of the site. In fact, restoration almost never progresses in this manner. Rather, multiple entries are more typically used to affect some of the complex changes that are often required. As restoration actions are planned and sequenced, it may be useful to represent the various anticipated steps as a series of intermediate phases, stages, or states in a diagram that describes the transition in greater detail (described in Section 6.4).

In the descriptions of the transitions that follow, we have also provided examples of possible changes for several of the transitions to illustrate how these changes might be characterized.

T1a: Reduce the cover of Wyoming big sagebrush, and increase the abundance and diversity of native bunchgrasses and forbs to acceptable levels.

Example: Reduce big sagebrush canopy cover from current levels (35%) to 5-15%.

Establish at least three large and one small native bunchgrasses at a cumulative cover of greater than 30%. Establish at least 12 native forbs and subshrubs, including species of *Lupinus, Achillea, Erigeron, Eriogonum,* and *Lomatium.*

T1b: Same as T1a, but also reduce weed abundance.

Example: Same as T1a, in addition to reducing cheatgrass cover from current levels (25%) to less than 1% and reducing average density to less than 3 plants/m^2.

T2: Increase the abundance and diversity of native bunchgrasses and/or forbs to acceptable levels. If weedy species are not extensive (not often the case) and if native diversity is high on or near the site, natural dispersal and succession may bring about this transition.

T3: Reduce the cover of rabbitbrush or other shrubs. Usually, this also involves increasing the abundance and diversity of native bunchgrasses and forbs and reducing weed abundance.

T4a: Reduce weed abundance, and increase native shrub and forb abundance and diversity.

T4b: Same as T4a, but do not include shrubs in the restoration, with the expectation that they will establish on their own.

T5a: Same as T4a, but also increase native bunchgrass abundance and diversity.

T5b: Same as T5a, but do not include shrubs in the restoration, with the expectation that they will establish on their own.

T6a: Reduce weed abundance, and increase native shrub, forb, and bunchgrass abundance and diversity.

T6b: Same as T6a, but do not include shrubs in the restoration, with the expectation that they will establish on their own.

T6c: Reduce weed abundance, and replace them with bunchgrasses only. Note that restoration of states IV and V could also proceed in a similar, bunchgrass-only transition to state RIII, with both shrubs and forbs not included.

TR3a: Increase forb abundance and diversity in a state consisting largely of native bunchgrasses.

TR3b: Increase shrub abundance in a state consisting largely of bunchgrasses only.

TR2: Increase shrub abundance in a state consisting largely of bunchgrasses and forbs.

TR1: Establish missing species, or alter the abundance of different species on the site to within the natural range of variability.

Example: Establish *Crepis atribarba, Elymus elymoides, Castilleja thompsonii, Mertensia longiflora, Saxifraga integrifolia,* and *Lomatium gormanii* at densities greater than 12 plants/hectare.

Table 1. Changes in major functional groups associated with transitions from starting states (T#) and transitions from restored states (TR#) (see Figure 4). X = necessary change, A = change as needed (depends on current composition and the likelihood of passive restoration bringing about transition).

Transition	Changes in Functional Groups				
	Reduce Shrubs	Control Invasives	Enhance Forbs	Enhance Bunchgrasses	Enhance Shrubs
T1a	X		X	X	
T1b	X	X	X	X	
T2			A	A	
T3	X	X	X		X
T4a		X	X		X
T4b		X	X		X
T5a		X	X	X	X
T5b		X	X	X	X
T6a		X	X	X	X
T6b		X	X	X	X
T6c		X	X	X	X
TR3a		A	X		X
TR3b		A			X
TR2		A	A		X
TR1		A	A	A	A

6. Restoration of Degraded Shrub-Steppe

6.1 Setting Restoration Goals

Many different possible restoration goals may be appropriate for degraded shrub-steppe, depending on how and for what purposes a site is managed. Future anticipated uses of a site often play a central role in shaping restoration goals, such as establishing high-quality nesting and brood-rearing habitat for sage-grouse. Goals may be further altered or constrained depending on the amount of funding available to carry out the restoration and other factors that may limit restoration alternatives. The restored state descriptions presented in Section 5.3 can provide a general characterization of a restoration goal, but goals usually need to be refined based on specific management needs or project focus. While it is impossible to anticipate all the potential goals managers may envision, we suggest some here that may encompass those managers might consider for shrub-steppe habitat types:

- Restore an ecologically resilient and resistant native shrub-steppe community.
- Restore key components to enhance high-quality habitat for sage-grouse.
- Restore native bunchgrasses and forbs to an abundance and diversity matching the natural range of variability of reference sites.
- Restore productive rangelands that also support a diversity of wildlife.

6.2 Assessing Site Conditions and Reference Sites

Most extant shrub-steppe in eastern Washington has been degraded or damaged to some extent due to a long history of land uses that have altered the historic vegetation structure, reduced abundance of native species, increased the abundance of system-altering nonnative species, altered physical conditions such as soil nutrient status and density, and removed biological crusts, to name just a few. Disturbance processes may have been altered as well (e.g., more ignition sources, greater fuel continuity, unsuitably high levels of grazing, or grazing at times of the year that native species cannot sustain). The nature and extent of this degradation varies considerably across the landscape, depending on both the causes and duration of factors that stressed the ecosystems.

This variability creates a diverse range of starting states that confront the land manager contemplating restoring a site. The initial assessment of the project site, its history, and surroundings will provide the information necessary to: (1) accurately identify which of the states identified in the STM represent the starting point of a particular restoration project (see Figure 4) and (2) begin to make key decisions regarding how restoration actions should proceed. Table 2 provides an overview of some factors that a site assessment may reveal and that may need to be considered in terms of their effects on restoration success.

Table 2. Site-related factors that may affect restoration outcomes and that should be assessed prior to commencing restoration activities.

Physical Conditions	Biological Conditions	Ecological Processes and Land Use	Historical Land Use	Landscape Context	Reference Site Assessment
Soil texture	Presence of weeds	Fire more frequent than historical natural range of variability	Residual herbicide	Adjacent land uses	Native species composition and abundance
Soil nutrient status	Shrub, bunchgrass, and forb abundance	Heavy grazing	Historical grazing	Extent and condition of sage-grouse habitat	
Soil depth	Shrub, bunchgrass, and forb diversity	Grazing seasonality	Historical cultivation	Presence of weeds nearby	
Compacted soils, erosion	Vegetation pattern and variability	Water or wind erosion			
Steep or rocky sites	Presence of planted cultivars				
Aspect and elevation	Allelopathic legacies				
Precipitation	Presence of intact biological crust				
Area					

Physical conditions: Moisture availability, which can be key in determining the likelihood of restoration success, can be affected by many physical factors in addition to the amount and seasonality of precipitation. Finer textured soils, deeper soils, north-facing slopes, and sites in areas with higher precipitation all can result in moister sites and a greater chance that seed will germinate and plugs will survive. Figure 5 presents a schematic interpretation of how several of these major physical conditions interact to affect the likelihood of restoration actions succeeding.

Sites with low precipitation are likely to experience frequent restoration failures. Similarly, sites with shallow soils may also be especially susceptible to drought conditions and less conducive to successful restoration. Heat load (McCune 2007), a parameter that integrates slope angle and aspect, is greatest on steep, southwest-facing slopes, where evapotranspiration and water stress are highest, thereby exacerbating droughtlike conditions. Where all three of these factors are near their most extreme (within box "A" in Figure 5), the likelihood of restoration being successful is significantly reduced. The probability of

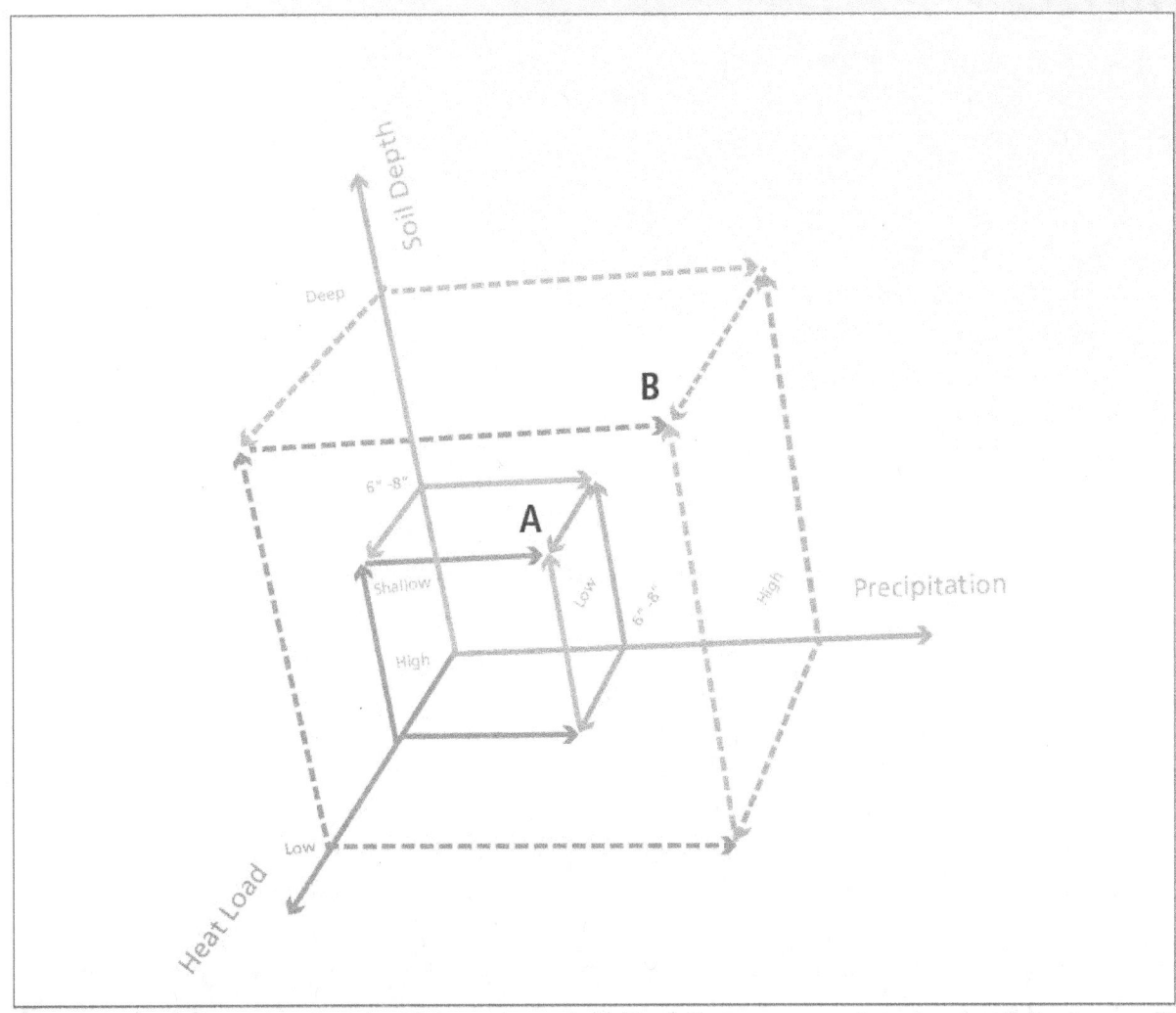

Figure 5. Hypothesized interactions of site physical characteristics on the likelihood of restoration success. Restoration is least likely to be successful within box "A," where shallow soils combine with low precipitation and high heat load to create particularly stressful conditions.

success increases as one moves outward on any axis and is greatest where high precipitation is combined with deep soils and low heat loads (point "B" in Figure 5).

Ideally, we would like to define the size and shape of a sector within Figure 5 that delineates conditions in which restoration should not be attempted due to the low probability of success. As a starting hypothesis, we suggest that areas with annual precipitation less than 6-8 inches (generally the lower limit for big sagebrush (Miller et al. 2011)), topsoil depths less than 6-8 inches, and high heat stress (steep south- or southwest-facing slopes) should be avoided. This sector is depicted as box "A" in Figure 5, although in reality it would be considerably more irregularly shaped, with the thresholds along each axis varying across a range of values as they interact in combination with each other. Other physical factors not shown in Figure 5 (e.g., soil texture, precipitation seasonality, average wind speeds, etc.) will further modify these threshold values.

Soil fertility will differentially affect the growth rates of both native and introduced species and should be considered when making species selections to include in seed mixes. Some plants, such as cheatgrass, which can alter soil nitrogen availability, can influence the success of restoration plantings (Booth, Stark, and Caldwell 2003; Sperry, Belnap, and Evans 2006). Other factors, such as compacted soils, slope steepness, rockiness, and proximity to roads (which also affect equipment accessibility to the site), also may influence restoration options.

Finally, clearly defining the area in which restoration will occur is fundamental. Determining the perimeter, as well as potential lines whereby the site may be subdivided into smaller parcels, can be important in making adjustments once a project is underway.

Biological conditions: The species and abundance of nonnative plants will greatly influence decisions regarding weed control techniques (e.g., biocontrols, herbicides, mechanical control). The abundance and diversity of native forbs, bunchgrasses, and shrubs will determine which species and the amount that need to be restored. Decisions on the content of seed mixes and sowing rates will depend on these assessments.

Shrubs on a site present issues that deserve special consideration. Although they usually are native species that are desirable to retain, an overabundance can prevent other natives from being established and may require special strategies to reduce. Furthermore, their presence can pose significant obstacles during the use of many types of seeding and cultivating equipment. Carefully mapping how this extant vegetation varies across the site is especially important in the restoration enhancement of extant shrub-steppe and poses some unique challenges that tend to be less of a problem in restoration of agricultural fields. Ignoring such variability and applying treatments uniformly across an entire project area may waste considerable resources either by applying them where they are unneeded or applying the treatments that will not accomplish the desired objectives.

If significant numbers of cultivars and nonnative species with desirable characteristics occur on a site, decisions must be made whether or not they should be retained and how this might affect restoration strategies and feasibility and how this could potentially alter longer term successional trajectories. Allelopathic residues, such as from knapweeds and some other plants (Ridenour and Callaway 2001), may hinder seed germination and establishment.

The presence and nature of biological crusts are also important features to note. Crusts can take many decades to develop, are difficult or impossible to restore, and can play a key role in limiting weed establishment and spread (Ponzetti, McCune, and Pyke 2007) and in the fixation of soil nitrogen (Evans and Belnap 1999). Disrupting biological soil crusts, when they exist, is generally undesirable and should be avoided whenever possible if restoration objectives can still be accomplished.

Ecological processes and land use: Oftentimes, disturbances and other ecological processes have departed significantly from their historical condition or natural range of variability. Some activities or ecological processes may need to be altered or corrected when they constrain the integrity of the native shrub-steppe ecosystems. Too frequent fire, inappropriate grazing practices, and recreational vehicle use are the principle factors that often need to be addressed before most other restoration actions can begin.

Historical land use: Legacies from past land uses on a site can require focused efforts to mitigate effects and can impact restoration actions and success. In degraded rangeland, past grazing practices and fire often have heavily influenced site conditions in ways that can affect restoration. Historical grazing can result in areas of localized soil compaction and weed hot spots, such as around salt block locations. Also, the composition and abundance of native species often has been dramatically altered by past grazing. Firebreaks constructed using excavation equipment in past fires, if not revegetated, may persist as avenues of weed infestation and require remediation, and the fires may have greatly altered shrub abundance, species composition, and the intactness of biological crusts. All of these legacies may have pushed the site into another stable state which, until these underlying conditions are modified, will never return to its original condition.

Landscape context: Potential impacts from lands surrounding restoration sites are important to consider. Herbicide drift from adjacent agricultural fields, vehicular activities, current and past livestock grazing, and weed infestations are some of the most common factors from adjacent sites that can influence restoration actions and likelihood of success. Also, many other factors of the larger landscape beyond the boundaries of the restoration site itself must be taken into consideration, especially when sage-grouse habitat is a primary driver behind restoration.

Reference site assessment: A more detailed picture of how sites might be restored can be obtained by examining reference sites. Nearby natural areas and native habitats that are relatively undisturbed can provide valuable insights about species composition, abundance, and site variability that can be used in designing restoration objectives. The physical features of restoration sites should be assessed, and similarities and differences within the project area should be noted to determine how directly analogous the sites may be. If reference sites are not available, ecological site descriptions (*http://efotg.sc.egov.usda.gov/treemenuFS. aspx*), which provide possible species composition and abundance information, can be obtained for many areas (see Section 3.4). Daubenmire's (1970) data and descriptions of shrub-steppe types can also be useful in providing supplementary information.

In summary, the assessment of site characteristics and conditions is essential to accurately identify factors that have contributed to the degradation of the site and to understand which key ecological components are missing or impaired, so that restoration can explicitly address these issues and deficiencies.

6.3 Defining Explicit Restoration Objectives

Information from the assessments of the site, together with comparisons to reference sites, are used to develop restoration objectives that will accomplish the overall restoration goals. Although most of the examples we examined in Washington involved restoration of potential shrub-steppe rather than enhancement of degraded habitat (as described in Section 1.2), development of restoration objectives should proceed in a similar manner for both types of restoration.

Typically, objectives are developed to add specificity to the restored states described in Section 5.3 in terms of four parameters: *species composition, abundance, vegetation structure, and distribution on the landscape.*

However, we found little uniformity in how managers have approached characterizing these parameters. Generally, objectives appeared to be, at best, only casually articulated and often had to be inferred from seed mixes used in planting. In the following sections, we suggest how greater rigor can be injected into defining objectives. Numerous references exist on setting appropriate objectives. Wirth and Pyke (2007) provide numerous examples and an extensive list of other references specifically for shrub-steppe ecosystems.

6.3.1 Setting Species Composition and Abundance Objectives

Consulting species lists that have been compiled from reference sites (Section 6.2) provides an important first step in defining composition objectives. While such lists may provide a basis for a long-term project objective, this rarely is appropriate for shorter term objectives. Instead, these objectives should reflect that restoring a full complement of shrub-steppe species is not an instantaneous, one-entry effort. Rather, it is a process that takes repeated interventions to control weeds and restore diverse species assemblages, allow natives to disperse in from adjacent areas, and develop biotic crusts.

As can be seen from the STM in Figure 4, several restored states are possible for any particular starting state, requiring that choices be made in terms of restoration objectives. In some cases, a decision to restore a site to a partially restored state (e.g., RII or RIII) may be made due to resource constraints, recognizing that moving an ecosystem into a more complex state may become feasible in the future with additional funds or other resources. In such situations, these states might simply be considered as moderate-term or interim objectives. In other cases, restoration to one of these states may satisfy management objectives and remain as the long-term goal.

Objectives pertaining to increasing the abundance of a species similarly must account for the time needed for perennials and shrubs to increase in cover and grow in stature and for species to reproduce and proliferate across a site. Understanding the rate and sequence of all of these steps is a difficult but critical part of successful, staged restoration that is based on principles of successional management. This process can be facilitated by establishing clear shorter term objectives. This is illustrated in the following series of objectives for a single, hypothetical site:

Year 1: Greater than 80% of all seeded species will be established on site. Cover of seeded bunchgrasses will be greater than 15%. Annual weeds will be less than 5% of total cover.

Year 3: All seeded species will be established. Bunchgrass cover will be greater than 35%. Annual weeds will be less than 2%.

Year 10: Greater than 80% of all species on the reference site species list will be present within the restoration area.

6.3.2 Setting Species Distribution Objectives

Incorporating spatially explicit components into objectives is particularly important in restoration enhancement of degraded shrub-steppe where natural variability of extant vegetation often is high. Unlike agricultural field restoration, where weed control treatments and seed mixes may be applied uniformly across entire sites, objectives for enhancing degraded shrub-steppe must recognize the often fundamentally different nature of the restoration process in these sites. For example, some weed infestations may only be concentrated in hot spots. Forb diversity or shrub density may be outside the natural range of variability only in particular areas. Thus, objectives often need to be carefully based on detailed maps generated in the site assessment to reflect not only the existing heterogeneity in species' distributions but also heterogeneity of physical features within the site that are reflected in the extant vegetation (e.g., local lithosol patches, swales, etc.). Objectives may need to be further refined to reflect differences across the site in what is feasible to accomplish as well. By refining objectives in this way, considerable savings can be realized by avoiding unnecessary or unproductive actions. Examples of distribution objectives for a hypothetical site might include:

> In zone A (20 acres), reduce big sagebrush density by 50%; establish tall bunchgrasses uniformly across zone; establish full suite of forbs in at least 10 patches. In zone B (20 acres), increase native forb diversity by establishing at least 10 patches of perennial forbs a, b, c, and x, y, z. In zone C (30 acres), reduce weed j to less than 2% cover, and establish tall bunchgrasses uniformly across zone to greater than 30% cover.

Distributional objectives may also reflect typical differences in species occurrence within shrub-steppe communities. For example, it may be appropriate to stipulate that native bunchgrasses be established at some target level of abundance across an entire site, whereas it may be acceptable that some forbs only occur in several patches somewhere on a site.

6.3.3 Setting Vegetation Structure Objectives

Having explicit structural objectives can be important for some situations and to meet some restoration objectives. For example, sage-grouse have particular structural requirements for different parts of their life cycle (see Section 3.6). Thus, a restoration goal of providing winter sage-grouse habitat at a site would necessitate having both compositional (e.g., big sagebrush) and structural (e.g., greater than 25 cm tall, greater than 15% canopy cover) objectives. Similarly, restoration of sage-grouse lek habitat might require only a structural objective (e.g., low, open grass), which could be met using native or nonnative bunchgrasses.

6.4 Identifying Needed Interventions

Once both the starting state of a site has been identified (Section 6.2) and the desired restored state has been chosen (Sections 6.3.1, 6.3.2, and 6.3.3), the appropriate transition connecting the two states can be identified from Figure 4. Thus, for example, if site assessments indicate a site is in Starting State V (dominated largely by cheatgrass with few native forbs), and it is determined that management objectives can be met by converting it to Restored State RII (dominated by native grassland with forbs), one can quickly see that the transition between these states is T5b. This transition will require controlling the cheatgrass and increasing the abundance and diversity of the bunchgrasses and forbs (1) that have been identified from reference communities, (2) that are deficient on the site in its current state, and (3) that have been chosen for restoration.

At this stage, it can be useful to add greater specificity regarding the needed biotic interventions. Identifying which species need to be added to a site to meet restoration objectives, identifying which particular weeds most need to be controlled, and describing the nature of their infestations (e.g., scattered individuals, several hot spots, etc.) all will be necessary information to use in deciding on the most appropriate treatments in Section 6.6.

For example, one approach to this could begin with a list of species from an appropriate ecological site description. Table 3 illustrates such a list for dry loamy soils in a zone with 9-15 inches of annual precipitation. The percentages following each species or species group are based on forage production rather than on a more ecologically meaningful measure, such as percent cover. However, the list can provide a rough idea of both the diversity and relative abundance of different species that might be included in a restoration. Note that some forbs are only identified to genus, so consultation with local experts may be necessary to identify which species are most appropriate at a particular site. This list can be compared with lists from nearby reference sites, which include the percent cover of locally occurring species, and from the site to be restored, to determine which species may already be present and which may be deficient or missing. This information can then be used to develop a preliminary list of species to include in restoration of the site. Further considerations of selecting species to be included in restoration mixes are discussed in Section 6.7.6.

Although not explicitly depicted in the STM in Figure 4, it must be recognized that some threats and physical site conditions (identified in Section 6.2 and Table 2) may contribute to a site remaining in its current, altered state. Such factors may require other types of interventions that abate the threats and/or correct limiting site factors. Relieving overgrazing, eliminating nearby sources of weeds, or loosening compacted soils are several such conditions that are frequently encountered in degraded shrub-steppe restoration.

Table 3. List of species, grouped by functional type, from a Natural Resources Conservation Service ecological site description of dry loamy soils in a zone with 9-15 inches of annual precipitation.

Ecological Site Number	Ecological Site Name			Below	Normal	Above
R008XY101WA	Dry Loamy 9-15 PZ		pounds/acre/year:	600	750	900

Historical Climax Plant Community

Plant Group Type

Perennial Cool Season Mid-Grass Decreasers		pound		
Count Each Listed Species up to the listed pounds for the Species				
PSSP6	bluebunch wheatgrass	540	72%	
POCU3	Cusick's bluegrass	50	7%	
FEID	Idaho fescue	9	1%	

Perennial Cool Season Mid-Grass Increasers		pound		
Count Each Listed Species up to the listed pounds for the Species				
POSE	Sandberg bluegrass	75	10%	
ACTH7	Thurber needlegrass	50	7%	
HECOC	needleandthread	18	2%	
KOMA	prairie Junegrass	7.5	1%	
ELEL5	bottlebrush squirreltail	7.5	1%	

Perennial Cool Season Tall-Grass		pound		
Count any Listed Species up to the listed pounds for the Species				
LECI4	basin wildrye	7.5	1%	

Annual Grasses		pound		
Count any Listed Species up to the listed pounds for the Species				
VUOC	sixweeks fescue	7.5	1%	

Shrubs/Deep Rooted/Non-Sprouters		60	pound	8%
Count any Listed Species up to the listed pounds for the Group				
ARTRW	Wyoming big sagebrush			
ARTRT	basin big sagebrush			

Shrubs/Deep Rooted/Sprouters		9	pound	1%
Count any Listed Species up to the listed pounds for the Group				
CHRYS	rabbitbrush			
ERNAN	rubber rabbitbrush			
CHVI8	green rabbitbrush			

Shrubs/Shallow Rooted/Sprouters		18	pound	2%
Count any Listed Species up to the listed pounds for the Group				
ARTR4	threetip sagebrush			

Shrubs/N-fixers		7.5	pound	1%
Count any Listed Species up to the listed pounds for the Group				
PUTR2	antelope bitterbrush			

Half Shrub		7.5	pound	1%
Count any Listed Species up to the listed pounds for the Group				
ERMI4	Weyth buckwheat			
ERNI2	snow buckwheat			
ERSP7	rock buckwheat			
ERHE2	parsnipflower buckwheat			
ERIOG	buckwheat			

Plant Group Type

Perennial Forbs/Fibrous-rooted		8	pound	1%
Count any Listed Species up to the Listed Pounds for the Group				
LIRU4	western gromwell			
PHLI	threadleaf phacelia			
MELO4	small bluebells			
ERPU2	shaggy fleabane			
RAGL	sagebrush buttercup			
CLPU	pinkfaries			
ERCO5	longleaf fleabane			
GAAR	common gaillardia			
MERTE	bluebells			
ARCO5	ballhead sandwort			
SYMPH	aster			

Perennial Forbs/taprooted		8	pound	1%
Count any Listed Species up to the Listed Pounds for the Group				
NOTR2	weevil microseris			
PHHO	spiny phlox			
CRAT	slender hawksbeard			
PHSP	showy phlox			
PHLOX	phlox			
PENST	penstemon			
AGGL	pale agoseris			
DENU2	Nuttal's larkspur			
COLI2	narrowleaf mountaintrumpet			
STST5	narrowleaf goldenweed			
PHLO2	longleaf phlox			
CRAC2	longleaf hawksbeard			
COGR4	largeflower mountaintrumpet			
ARHO2	Holboell's rockcress			

Perennial Forbs/thickened taproot		9	pound	1%
Count any Listed Species up to the Listed Pounds for the Group				
BASA3	arrowleaf balsamroot			
LOTR2	nineleaf biscuitroot			
LOMAT	lomatium			
LOGO	Gorman's biscuitroot			
LODI	fernleaf biscuitroot			
BACA3	Carey's balsamroot			
BALSA	balsamroot			

Perennial Forbs/N-fixers		18	pound	2%
Count any Listed Species up to the Listed Pounds for the Group				
LUSU5	sulphur lupine			
LUPIN	lupine			
ASPU9	woollypod milkvetch			
ASMI9	weedy milkvetch			
LUSE4	silky lupine			
ASTRA	milkvetch			
OXYTR	crazyweed			

Spring bulbs & Ephemerals		8	pound	1%
Count any Listed Species up to the Listed Pounds for the Group				
FRPU2	yellow misionbells			
ALLIU	wild onion			
TRGR7	wild hyacinth			
CALOC	Mariposa lily			
LIGL2	bulbous woodlandstar			

Perennial Forbs/parasitic to semi-parasitic		8	pound	1%
Count any Listed Species up to the Listed Pounds for the Group				
CATH4	Thompson's Indian paintbrush			
CASTI2	Indian paintbrush			
COUM	bastard toadflax			

biennial		8	pound	1%
Count any Listed Species up to the Listed Pounds for the Group				
CHDO	Douglas' dustymaiden			

Annual Forbs		9	pound	1%
Count any Listed Species up to the Listed Pounds for the Group				
ERLI	desert yellow fleabane			
COPA3	smallflower blue eyed Mary			
ERIGE2	fleabane			

Perennial Forbs-Stoloniferous		8	pound	1%
Count any Listed Species up to the Listed Pounds for the Group				
ANDI2	low pussytoes			

The additional detailed information gathered in this section can also be useful in beginning to break down the restoration transition into a series of steps, which may be accomplished separately or combined when possible to reduce costly entries on a site. To visualize these steps, it may be helpful to create a diagram depicting hypothesized intermediate stages or phases in the transition between the starting and restored states, such as illustrated in a hypothetical example in Figure 6.

6.5 Assessing Project Feasibility

Understanding logistical and other factors that could constrain a project is important in initiating and successfully completing a site restoration. This information can be gathered and incorporated at various stages during project development. It can be especially useful to do this once restoration objectives have been defined and interventions have been identified, since one can then reassess the feasibility of a project by examining available resources and other factors that may put additional sideboards on the scale of a project. Factors that often constrain restoration projects fall into three

principal areas. These include funding, manpower and equipment availability, and seed availability. By carefully considering these factors and how they may influence project outcomes, objectives can then be reassessed to ensure they remain realistic.

Funding: The amount of funding available to support restoration usually is limited. Furthermore, the duration of such funding often is relatively short. Since most restoration projects require multiple entries over several years, caution should be exercised in undertaking projects if uninterrupted, long-term support is unlikely to be forthcoming. It is also critical to recognize that cutting corners to save money may compromise the success of the overall project. Insufficient weed control, often resulting from too few treatments, wrong herbicide selection, or inappropriate herbicide use are all a frequent false economy. Projects also frequently fall short and fail to meet objectives when seed mixes that are not locally adapted or that are deficient in species or functional group diversity are used.

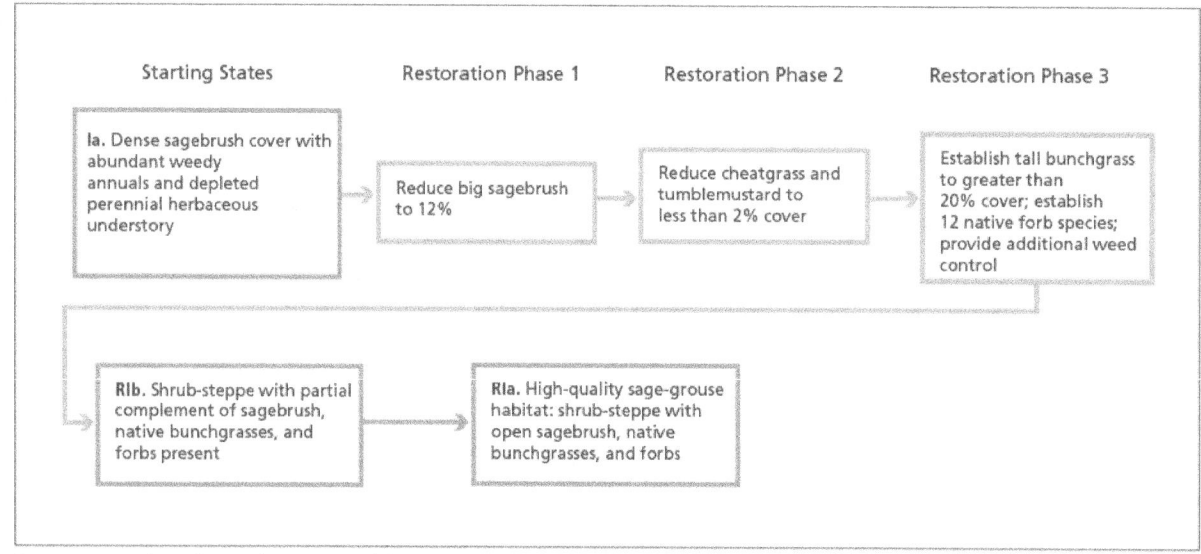

Figure 6. Hypothetical, staged restoration of shrub-steppe Starting State 1b (from Figure 4). The transition T1b to Restored State R1b is proposed to take place in three phases, beginning with the reduction in big sagebrush cover, followed by controlling invasive weeds. Establishing bunchgrasses and selected forbs, combined with additional weed control, completes the transition to R1b. The transition (TR1) to a high-quality sage-grouse habitat with a high diversity of forbs occurs through passive restoration.

Manpower and equipment: Having the appropriate equipment and manpower available when they are most needed can spell the difference between successful projects and well-intended failures. Herbicide applications should be timed correctly to achieve successful weed control. Seeds should also be sowed at the correct depths, at the right time of year, to achieve ideal germination rates. At times, savings can be realized by using equipment that is already owned or that can be readily borrowed (see Section 6.7.7). However, know the capabilities and limitations of this equipment to ensure planned treatments actually can be implemented using available resources.

Seed availability: Often, desired seed of locally adapted native species is unavailable, cannot be purchased in the desired quantities, or may only be obtained with significant advance notice. Projects should be carefully planned well in advance to collect native seed for nursery grow out or to allow growers to produce the needed quantities of all species. Alternatively, the species restoration list that was generated in Section 6.4 may need to be significantly revised based on this additional information.

The assessment described in this section is critical to ensure that a project's objectives are realistic and that the means to attain them are feasible. However, as treatments are decided upon and implemented, results are monitored and evaluated, and as adaptive management of the project progresses, this step should be regularly revisited to reexamine and (if necessary) revise both objectives and treatment strategies to be certain they remain feasible.

6.6 Decision Tree for Shrub-Steppe Restoration

Numerous factors need to be considered in determining which treatments will be most likely to successfully bring about the transition of a site from a starting state to a desired restored condition. Many of these factors have been reviewed in the previous sections. Here, we bring together these considerations into a coherent decisionmaking sequence using a decision tree (see Figure 7). This approach uses much of the information gathered about a potential restoration site to make decisions about appropriate strategies for moving ahead with a restoration project. At each step in the tree, a yes/no decision is made. Depending on the answer, one either moves on to

Photo by Matt Lavin

make another decision or is directed to take particular actions before moving on.

In this tree, decisions about which restoration treatments to choose are made beginning in step 7 and are examined in detail in Section 6.7. However, other information gathered during site assessments can strongly influence these decisions and are considered in the first six decisions of the tree.

The following points refer to the first seven numbered steps in the decision tree depicted in Figure 7.

(1) Close examination of a site may indicate that an ecological threshold has not been crossed, and, in time, succession may be expected to return a site to its natural range of variability. This may be the case, for example, with some sites in State II (e.g., sparse sagebrush with depleted understory - Figure 4). In such sites, restoration may not be necessary, although managers still may decide to proceed with restoration if it is deemed the recovery rate is unacceptably slow.

(2) Some ecological processes, such as too frequent fire, may have created a degraded state where an ecological threshold has been crossed or may have developed conditions that are extremely difficult to correct. It is usually pointless to carry out expensive restoration actions that will be undone by threats that have not been abated. However, some habitat components, such as bunchgrasses and shrubs, may be resilient to some types of disturbances and may be worth restoring anyway, if they confer important ecological benefits.

(3) and (3a) The probability of failure of many seeding and plugging treatments increases significantly in sites where annual precipitation totals fall below 6-8 inches/year and irrigation is not possible (see Figure 5). While restoration is still feasible in these sites, managers must recognize and plan for the constraints and risks these conditions pose.

(4) Deeper soils tend to retain moisture better and may increase the likelihood of seedling survival (see Figure 5). Finding suitable plant materials to use for restoration in sites with shallow, rocky soils and lithosols may be difficult, and the risk of poor germination and survival is likely to be higher.

(5) Treatments to enhance degraded shrub-steppe attempt to retain extant native species and biological crusts and generally avoid extensive use of highly disruptive actions (e.g., plowing, harrowing, etc.) used in the full field restoration of agricultural lands described in the WDFW shrub-steppe restoration manual (Benson et al. 2011). However, where there are few native species remaining on a site, such as State VI (Figure 4) and in other starting states that are highly degraded, it may be considerably more efficient to accept some loss of native plants and start over entirely using these more aggressive agricultural techniques. The term "significant" in this decision point is subjective and can refer to several different situations. It may be important to retain native species that are difficult to propagate if they remain on a site. Or, a diverse but sparse assemblage of native species might provide valuable natural sources for repopulating many native species. Alternatively, if the native species are concentrated in discrete areas, these may be left as undisturbed islands, while the remainder of the site is restored using the agricultural approaches.

(5a) A special case occurs in some former Conservation Reserve Program sites where nonnative bunchgrasses may have been used in the revegetation (particularly if biotic crusts, native forbs, and/or shrubs may also have begun

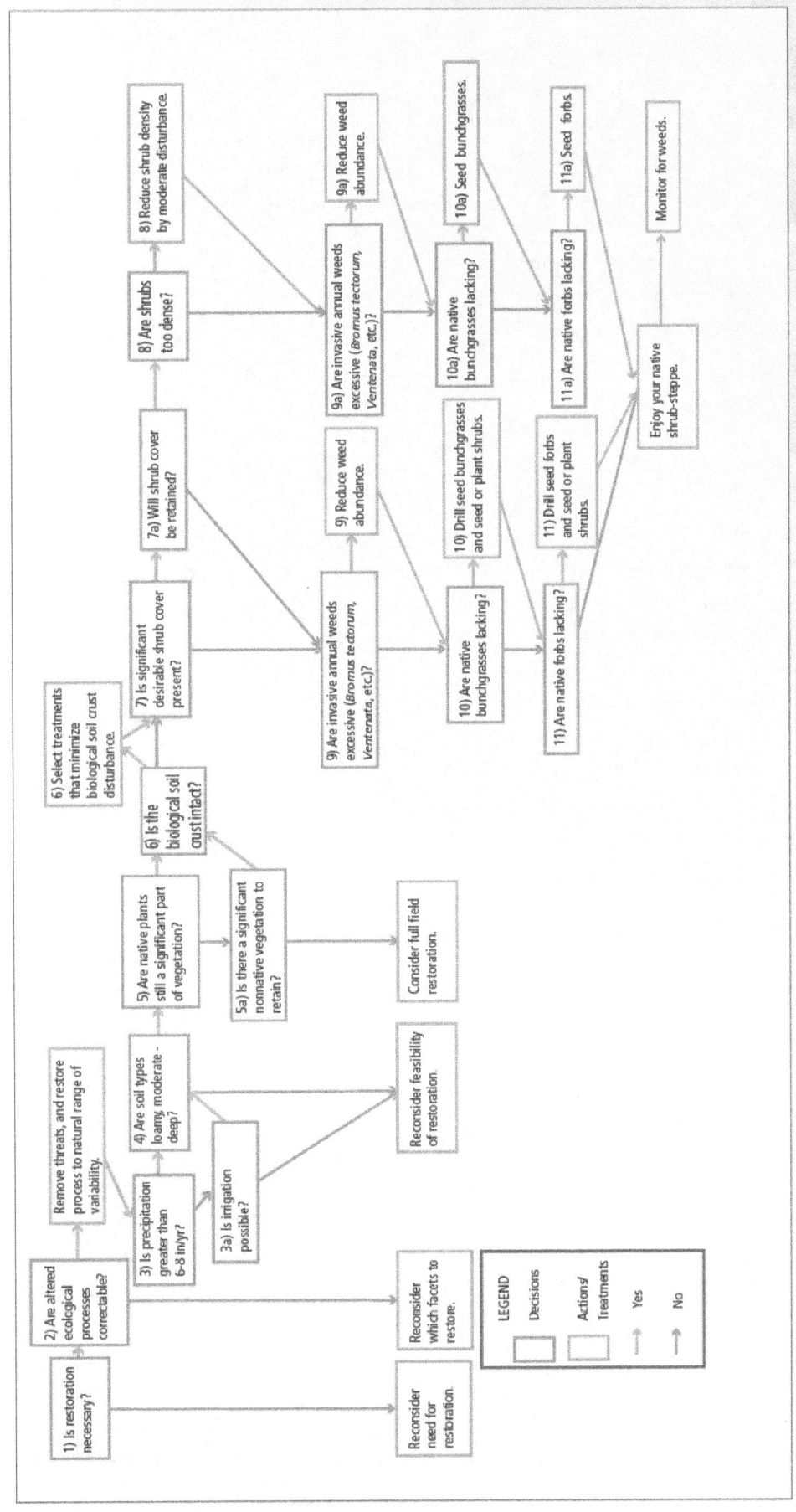

Figure 7. Decision tree for enhancing degraded shrub-steppe. Decisions 1-7 relate to general considerations based on site assessments and are described in Section 6.6. Decisions 8-11 regard choices of restoration treatments and are discussed in Section 6.7.

to reestablish). If the nonnative grasses function similarly to native species, it may be desirable to retain them rather than remove them and start anew.

(6) If a biological soil crust is present and largely intact, restoration treatments selected in steps 7-11 should be prioritized so they result in minimal disturbance to the biological soil crust (see Section 5.1).

(7) and (7a) This is a major decision point, as the presence of abundant desirable shrubs on a site presents conditions that can greatly limit potential restoration treatment alternatives. Retaining large numbers of mature shrubs on a site usually precludes the use of much ground-based machinery (tractor-drawn drill seeders, harrows, boom sprayers, etc. used in treatment steps 9-11). Alternative treatments that avoid disrupting the shrubs (steps 9a-11a) often are more costly and less likely to be successful. However, as noted in Section 3.6, large Wyoming big sagebrush plants are a critical component of sage-grouse habitat that can take decades to restore and, if present on a site, generally, should be preserved in most restoration efforts. Other shrubs, such as threetip sagebrush, rabbitbrush species, bitterbrush, hopsage, horsebrush, and several other species that may be locally important, also may take many years to reach mature size. Deciding what constitutes a "significant" shrub cover and whether or not to retain it will depend on several factors: (a) the species, age, and abundance of the shrubs; (b) the loss in ecological benefits should they be removed; (c) the loss of these ecological benefits until restored shrubs reach a similar size and abundance; (d) the costs of removing the shrubs; and (e) the reduced cost and increased probability of restoration success in the absence of shrubs, balanced against the greater cost of restoration with shrubs present.

6.7 Identifying Restoration Treatments

Shrub-steppe restoration is still very much in its infancy as an ecological science. Accounts of particular treatment combinations resulting in restoration successes are largely anecdotal, and accounts of failures and the factors that may have contributed to them are absent from the published literature and difficult to extract from practitioners. Rigorous experiments testing treatments against one another are few, and studies that have applied treatments uniformly across multiple sites (and which thereby might permit broader generalization of results) are almost nonexistent (Pyke et al. 2011).

In Washington, as in most of the arid West, restoration has largely focused on full field restoration, transforming agricultural fields, Conservation Reserve Program lands, and rangeland that has been severely degraded to a more native condition. Full field restoration has drawn on the extensive experience of the agricultural community to use agricultural equipment and approaches to control weeds and establish desirable vegetation. In recent years, considerable advances have been made in adapting and developing new equipment that can be used in rangelands for revegetating and restoring these rougher habitats. The Rangeland Technology and Equipment Council (Wiedemann 2007) is an excellent source for much current information on alternative technologies and approaches, and much of these are directly relevant to the restoration discussed in this section.

Nevertheless, up until now, considerably less effort has been directed at enhancing degraded shrub-steppe while trying to retain extant native vegetation. These situations present enormous challenges to traditional agricultural approaches. Many types of equipment are unusable where rocky soils, rough terrain, or large shrubs limit access. Furthermore, a desire to avoid disrupting intact soil crusts and extant native species generally discourages customary approaches, which typically involve widespread tilling and use of broad-spectrum herbicides.

However, recent research is strongly urging managers to renew a focus on restoring ecosystems that retain remnant native species (McIver et al. 2010; Davies and Sheley 2011). Given the high costs and frequent failures encountered when seeding native species in arid environments, researchers are increasingly recommending that managers explore restoration of sites where natives are still present (Rafferty and Young 2002). Thus, we expect significant progress will be made in this field in the next several years.

In this section, we examine a variety of approaches that provide potential guidance for selecting effective treatments for restoring extant shrub-steppe. After reviewing several basic principles for developing restoration strategies (Section 6.7.1), we consider the many potential combinations of treatments grouped under several categories. These categories span the major challenges encountered in shrub-steppe enhancement, including: reducing sagebrush abundance where it has exceeded its natural range of variability (Section 6.7.2); controlling invasive weeds (Section 6.7.3); increasing the abundance and diversity of native grasses, forbs, and shrubs where shrubs are absent (Section 6.7.4); and increasing grasses and forbs where shrubs are present (Section 6.7.5). In each section, various alternative treatments are presented in groups ranked with a high-, medium-, or low-likelihood of success. These rankings are based on evidence from the field, where it exists, and on our best estimates according to our ecological experience with these ecosystems. We also present other potential alternatives that may be feasible in the future, but which have so far received little or no field testing. In a separate section, we discuss considerations for selecting species to include in restoration projects (Section 6.7.6). We conclude this section with a discussion of the relative costs of different treatment methods (Section 6.7.7).

6.7.1 Restoration Principles

In this section, we suggest three principles that we consider fundamental in developing successful strategies for enhancing degraded shrub-steppe:

(1) **Approach restoration from a successional management perspective.**
Considerable innovation has occurred in the last several years in melding ecological theory with weed control practices (Cox and Anderson 2004; Krueger-Mangold, Sheley, and Svejcar 2006). The use of natural successional processes in restoration efforts is a new conceptual paradigm to range management and suggests new approaches for controlling weeds and restoring degraded habitats. Two tables from Krueger-Mangold, Sheley, and Svejcar (2006) are reproduced in Tables 4 and 5, and they summarize the salient points of this approach, which focuses on tailoring restoration practices to influence factors affecting three primary areas—site availability, species availability, and species performance. In restoration actions, considering these factors involves how they relate both to weed species that are being controlled and to establishing native species. These concepts are elaborated more fully in a number of recent papers coauthored by Sheley and others (see full list in References section).

Table 4. Causes of succession, contributing processes and components, and modifying factors (reproduced from Krueger-Mangold, Sheley, and Svejcar (2006)).

Causes of succession	Process and components	Modifying factors
Site availability	Disturbance	Size, severity, time intervals, patchiness, predisturbance history
Species availability	Dispersal	Dispersal mechanisms and landscape features
	Propagule pool	Land use, disturbance interval, species life history
Species performance	Resource supply	Soil, topography, climate, site history, microbes, litter retention
	Ecophysiology	Germination requirements, assimilation rates, growth rates, genetic differentiation
	Life history	Allocation, reproduction timing and degree
	Stress	Climate, site history, prior occupants, herbivory, natural enemies
	Interference	Competition, herbivory, allelopathy, resource availability, predators

Table 5. Causes of succession, contributing processes and components, and modifying factors in the expanded successional management framework. Successional models and relevant citations are listed in italics under processes. Bold-faced modifying factors are additional modifying factors proposed in text (reproduced from Krueger-Mangold, Sheley, and Svejcar (2006)).

Causes of succession	Processes and components	Modifying factors
Site availability	Disturbance *Tolerance (Connell and Slatyer 1977); Fluctuating Resource Availability (Davis et al. 2000)*	Size, severity, time intervals, patchiness, predisturbance history, **shallow tillage, grazing with multiple types of livestock**
Species availability	Dispersal *Inhibition (Connell and Slatyer 1977); Initial Floristic Composition (Egler 1954)*	Dispersal mechanisms and landscape features, dispersal vectors, **seedbed preparation, seeding in phases**
	Propagule pool *Inhibition, Initial Floristic Composition*	Land use, disturbance interval, species life history, **assessment of propagule pool, seed coating**
Species performance	Resource supply *Facilitation (Connell and Slatyer 1977); Resource Ratio Hypothesis (Tilman 1977, 1982, 1984, 1988)*	Soil, topography, climate, site history, microbes, litter retention, **soil resource assessment, soil impoverishment, resource use**
	Ecophysiology *Vital Attributes (Noble and Slatyer 1980)*	Germination requirements, assimilation rates, growth rates, genetic differentiation, **comparison between native and introduced environments, seed priming**
	Life history *Tolerance K- and r-strategists (MacArthur 1962)*	Allocation, reproduction timing and degree, **sensitivity analysis**
	Stress *Tolerance, C-S-R (Grime 1979); Community Assembly Theory (Diamond 1975)*	Climate, site history, prior occupants, herbivory, natural enemies **identifying abiotic and biotic filters, seeding species-rich mixtures**
	Interference *Inhibition*	Competition, herbivory, allelopathy, resource availability, predators other level interactions, **cover crops, assisted succession**

Several points related to this first principle have significant implications on restoration practices and are worth noting here. These have been particularly highlighted in ecological theory throughout the last several decades and are now beginning to be incorporated into restoration and land management (Jacobs, Carpinelli, and Sheley 1999). They include:

(a) Restoration failures are most often due to competition for safe sites for seeds.

(b) Competition for safe sites for seeds occurs because establishment and survival during the seedling stage is generally the most important period in the growth of plants on a site (site availability).

(c) To be successful, seedlings must find suitable safe sites in which to germinate (site and species availability).

(d) Seeds must be available in sufficient quantities so that many find their way into safe sites (species availability).

(e) Those species that can most quickly capture resources will survive (species performance). Without specific actions taken to address all of these factors, weeds usually prevail over natives because typical rangeland disturbances create safe sites especially suited to weeds, weeds generally produce far more seeds than natives, and weeds usually are better competitors and are able to quickly exploit resources.

(2) Adaptive management is the most promising approach for solving complex problems.

Recent research has characterized restoration challenges in arid rangeland ecosystems as fundamentally different from many other types of restoration and management actions. In other ecosystems, the relationships among variables are relatively constant, and the restoration outcomes are more predictable (Boyd and Svejcar 2009). Especially in arid ecosystems, relationships often are highly variable across space and time, the outcomes tend to be equally variable, and hence, solutions to these problems similarly vary across space and time. Such problems are referred to as "complex" and require different approaches than have traditionally been used to address "simple" problems with less inherent variability. Increasingly, adaptive management is being recommended as an effective approach for resolving these types of complex problems (Boyd and Svejcar 2009). Although the concept of adaptive management has been around for decades, there are surprisingly few examples of its successful application. Several recent publications have attempted to provide guidance for its use in restoration and management, such as a paper by Reever Morghan, Sheley, and Svejcar (2006), which describes the application of adaptive management in rangeland restoration.

This second principle also has significant implications for restoration practices that are worth noting here:

> (a) Specific prescriptions for restoration treatments are likely to have widely varied outcomes when applied at different times and places.

> (b) The large uncertainties associated with treatment outcomes make it extremely difficult to attach meaningful probabilities to the likelihood of success of restoration treatments.

> (c) Uncertainties are magnified further when multiple treatments are applied to address complex problems.

(3) Follow-up management is critical.

This principle derives directly from the previous one. By incorporating adaptive management into restoration projects, feedback from regular monitoring will readily identify where treatments failed to produce expected results. This information, in turn, can be used to design followup treatments to redirect successional trajectories that will move conditions further toward restoration objectives. When applied regularly during the course of a project, this approach will keep small problems from becoming colossal failures and will reduce costs and inefficiencies that inevitably result from working in complex ecosystems with high uncertainties.

There are important implications related to this third principle as well:

> (a) Plan from the outset to regularly monitor results and modify results with followup treatment strategies.

> (b) However, seek out opportunities to combine treatments.

There are two main sources of failure in restoration projects. The first was noted in the first principle and relates to competition for safe sites and resources between weeds and desired species. These are density-dependent factors, many of which can be modified directly or indirectly by management actions. The second includes density-independent factors, such as climate, herbivory, and wildfires, over which managers may have little or no control. These factors contribute immensely to the unpredictability of treatment outcomes. Such uncertainties cannot be overcome, but projects can avoid succumbing to unanticipated impacts by regular monitoring to detect failures and timely interventions to correct them (Sheley et al. 2010).

The big challenge is to minimize multiple entries as much as possible in order to keep costs down. Combining treatments where possible is one approach to reducing such costs, but there will always be a tension between the need for additional interventions in response to adaptive management and the need to rein in restoration costs. Seeding multiple species in a single application, such as sowing bunchgrasses with a variety of broadleaf species and even shrubs, is a frequently used combination treatment. It can be relatively straightforward using broadcast seeders but usually requires specialized equipment when drill seeding.

6.7.2 Reducing Shrub Abundance in Overly Dense Stands

Stands of shrubs that exceed the natural range of variability can develop in overgrazed rangeland, where Wyoming big sagebrush may become excessively dense and tall (Starting States Ia and Ib from Figure 4). In such cases, the stand is usually associated with a depauperate and often weedy understory (Starting State Ib from Figure 4). A first step in restoring such stands generally requires reducing the shrub density, which can be important in releasing understory species. In many instances, reducing rather than entirely removing the shrubs may be most desirable in order to preserve important habitat values (Stevens and Monsen 2004; Davies et al. 2009; Connelly, Rinkes, and Braun 2011). For example, the Sagebrush Steppe Treatment Evaluation Project (SageSTEP) (McIver et al. 2010) is a large-scale, multisite study that involves various treatments (e.g., herbicide, burning, and mechanical treatments) to reduce sagebrush canopy cover, but only preliminary results, which follow, have been reported so far (Pyke et al. 2011).

High-Likelihood Treatments

Herbicide: Aerial application of tebuthiuron (Spike 20P) pellets has been used to thin stands of big sagebrush (Olson, Hansen, and Whitson 1996; Blumenthal et al. 2006; Dahlgren, Chi, and Messmer 2006; McIver et al. 2010). The SageSTEP project applied this herbicide at a relatively low rate of 1-1.5 lb/acre to reduce sagebrush cover by about 50% and stimulate the herbaceous understory. This approach has been used to enhance sage-grouse habitat elsewhere (Dahlgren, Chi, and Messmer 2006) and was successful in reducing Wyoming big sagebrush at most sites in the SageSTEP project, including at the Moses Coulee Preserve in Washington. However, this approach can result in extensive spread of weedy species on the site, such as cheatgrass, if other control measures are not also applied (Blumenthal et al. 2006).

Tebuthiuron has been used to effectively reduce a variety of woody species, including *Chrysothamnus viscidiflorus* and *Tetradymia canescens*, but not *Chrysothamnus nauseosus* (Clary, Goodrich, and Smith 1985). 2,4-Dichlorophenoxyacetic acid (2,4-D) also has been widely used to control sagebrush (Johnson 1958), but damage to desirable, nontarget broadleaf species is often unacceptable. Similar damage to forbs can occur if tebuthiuron is used at higher concentrations (Pyke 2011).

Mechanical: Numerous types of equipment have been employed to remove shrubs from rangeland. Many are illustrated and described in the Revegetation Equipment Catalog website (*http://reveg-catalog.tamu. edu/04-Mechanical.htm*). Two of the most commonly used methods in Washington include:

- Chains pulled between two tractors have been used extensively for removing many types of woody vegetation. Various modifications to chains have been developed that affect the amount of ground disturbance. Depending on vegetation size and site objectives, it may be appropriate to use this technique either to break off many of the shrubs or to uproot them entirely. Most applications of chaining result in considerable damage to understory vegetation.

- Several types of rotary and flail mowers can be used to cut shrubs at various heights, depending on site objectives. For the SageSTEP project, a tractor-drawn rotary mower was used to cut sagebrush at a height of approximately 12 inches to reduce but not entirely remove shrubs. Others (Davies et al. 2009) have found that mowing sagebrush to approximately 8 inches resulted in long-term (greater than 20 years) reductions in abundance.

Moderate-Likelihood Treatments

Burning: Prescribed burning can be effective for meeting various types of shrub control objectives. Results vary considerably, depending on many factors, only some of which are easily controlled. Weather, season of burn, and ignition patterns will influence burn intensity, which in turn affects the severity and heterogeneity of burn impacts. Intense fires can result in complete kill of big sagebrush within a burned area, as well as significant damage to native plants and biological crusts in the understory (Davies et al. 2012). Other shrub species may resprout after fire (e.g., threetip sagebrush, rabbitbrush species), resulting in shorter term impacts (Daubenmire 1970). The SageSTEP project used a single prescribed burn treatment to reduce big sagebrush cover. The ability to control the amount of shrub removal, potential impacts (both positive and negative) to other species, and availability of trained crews to conduct the burns are all considerations that influence decisions regarding the utility of burn treatments.

Potential Treatments

Livestock grazing: Livestock have been used to reduce sagebrush abundance, either through mechanical breakage of the shrubs by trampling or by training cattle, sheep, or goats to preferentially browse on shrubs. Fred Provenza, Utah State University professor, is a leading advocate in this field and has published extensively on influencing animal behavior to selectively impact particular species of vegetation. His group has particularly focused on big sagebrush. One study is using fall grazing to modify the structure of sagebrush stands (*https://extension.usu.edu/behave/htm/current-projects/eating-sagebrush*). Although these practices have not been widely adopted in restoration of sagebrush habitats to date (Pyke 2011), they show potential promise for influencing vegetation composition and structure under some conditions.

6.7.3 Controlling Invasive Weeds

Extensive literature exists for controlling invasive weeds in rangelands, generally with a strong emphasis on comprehensive, multipronged approaches that incorporate integrated pest management. When we consider this literature in the context of enhancing shrub-steppe with extant native species, and incorporate principles of successional management, several important aspects are particularly worth noting:

(1) Weed management must be considered hand-in-hand with establishment of native species. Failure to successfully replace the spaces occupied by invasives with other desirable species will inevitably result in rapid reinfestation of habitats. Therefore, although weed control is discussed in its own section here, it is critical for all of these weed control treatments to be regarded as pieces of multitool treatment combinations that accomplish broader restoration goals.

(2) The importance of retaining extant native species and intact biological soil crusts can impose constraints that, at times, limit using some of the approaches normally available in integrated pest management. Some herbicides, for example, may have unacceptable impacts to desirable native species. Similarly, some equipment and techniques, such as tilling and disking large areas, are generally to be avoided for the same reasons.

(3) Herbicides are an important tool in controlling weeds in shrub-steppe restoration, but there are constraints and unknowns that must be taken into consideration when deciding on their use. Government agencies differ in terms of which herbicides are authorized for use and may limit the use of some described here. Also, impacts of many herbicides on native species in rangeland settings are poorly known. For example, almost no studies have examined herbicide impacts on biological soil crusts (Belnap et al. 2001). Therefore, caution must always be exercised when using herbicides in shrub-steppe

restoration. A summary of many herbicides used in this context is presented in (Benson et al. 2011).

With these caveats in mind, we primarily consider treatments in this section that appear to have limited impacts on native species and soil crusts. However, the potential for such impacts varies widely, and some negative impacts may be deemed to be acceptable "collateral damage." Such decisions need to be made based on local site considerations, direct observations of impacts, and restoration objectives.

We consider two main categories of invasive species in shrub-steppe—annual grasses and broadleaf forbs. While we focus this discussion on the problem species most frequently encountered in degraded Wyoming big sagebrush/bluebunch wheatgrass habitats in Washington, individual situations will vary considerably, depending on the biological and physical characteristics of the site, the particular weedy species involved, the nature of the infestations, the accessibility of the site, and the resources available.

Annual Grasses (particularly cheatgrass, but to some extent medusahead and ventenata)

High-Likelihood Treatments

Herbicides: Several herbicides have been used to reduce cheatgrass infestations with varying success. In shrub-steppe settings, depending on the nature of the infestations and the size of the site, applications can be made using manual equipment, boom sprayers on tractors or all-terrain vehicles, or aerially. Generally, ground-based methods are more effective.

> (1) Glyphosate (Roundup) is a broad-spectrum herbicide that can significantly reduce cheatgrass infestations when applied at low rates (6-12 oz/acre) in late winter or early spring (*http://ipm.montana.edu/cropweeds/ montguides/Cheatgrass.pdf*). However, use of this approach in Washington has shown mixed results (Lopushinsky, Strathmann, and Ross

personal communications – Appendix 1). Because glyphosate will affect most species, it is important to apply when desirable vegetation is largely dormant. Cheatgrass tends to germinate in the fall and early spring before many native species and, thus, presents a window for treatment when little else will be affected.

(2) Imazapic (Plateau) is a moderately persistent herbicide that provides both pre- and post-emergent control of several annual grasses (including cheatgrass) but can also affect some perennial grasses and broadleaf plants. Davison and Smith (2007) applied it at a rate of 105 grams/hectare to eliminate nonnative forbs and significantly reduce cheatgrass for 2 years without affecting native plants in Nevada. However, Ross (personal communication – Appendix 1) reported severe damage to desirable species with applications of 210-280 grams/hectare of imazapic in Washington. A study by Davies and Sheley (2011) showed significant control of medusahead with imazapic and imazapic plus burning treatments for 2 years, with the use of 87.5 grams/hectare of imazapic. The study also showed increases in native perennials. For SageSTEP, imazapic (68-92 grams/ hectare) was used to control cheatgrass as part of broader treatment combinations. Cheatgrass was significantly reduced for 3 years. However, slight reductions were observed in native perennial bunchgrasses, and native forbs were significantly reduced (SageSTEP 2010; Pyke et al. 2011). Baker, Garner, and Lyon (2009) applied imazapic at a high rate (175 grams/hectare) to control cheatgrass in big sagebrush sites in Colorado, but observed only a 67% decline in cheatgrass, with large negative impacts on native forbs. Control of ventenata with imazapic was tested in Washington (*http:// county.wsu.edu/whitman/agriculture/plants/weeds/ Documents/VentenataEB2040Epdf.pdf*), which showed better control is attained with spring rather than fall applications. The potential for nontarget effects on both broadleaf weeds and native species

necessitates further testing of this treatment before widespread application on a site that contains many desirable species. Lower application rates may avoid some of these nontarget effects.

(3) Imazapic plus glyphosate (Journey): Combinations of these two herbicides are also reported to afford control of cheatgrass. Cautions about potential impacts to native species are similar to the cautions mentioned with the use of imazapic.

Combined burning with imazapic: Evidence from several sites in Washington (SageSTEP 2010; Link and Hill 2011) and other states (Davies and Sheley 2011) support the use of prescribed fire followed by application of imazapic to control cheatgrass for several years. Where compared directly, the combined treatments outperformed burning or imazapic alone.

Moderate-Likelihood Treatments

Burning: Studies in Washington by Evans and Lih (2005) and Link et al. (2004) both confirm reports from other regions that hot fires generally result in reductions in cheatgrass abundance by consuming large quantities of seed. However, light fires may do little by themselves to reduce cheatgrass abundance, and regardless, reductions tend to be short lived. Cheatgrass repopulation of burned areas can be very rapid, primarily from prolific seed production. Burning would be most effective for controlling weeds when used as part of a more integrated approach that also incorporates herbicides.

Low-Likelihood Treatments

Herbicide: Sulfometuron-methyl (Oust) showed considerable promise for controlling cheatgrass in several studies conducted in the late 1990s (Pellant, Kaltenecker, and Jirik 1999). However, subsequent issues with crop damage due to offsite impacts resulted in multiple costly legal claims, and there is virtually no mention of this herbicide in rangeland literature in the past decade. Until these nontarget issues are clarified, there appears to be little likelihood of its use in rangeland settings. It

is reported to not perform well where soil pH is greater than 7 (Benson, personal communication - Appendix 1).

Mowing: Generally, there is little evidence that mowing provides significant control of cheatgrass or other annual grasses in most rangeland settings. A sufficient number of plants usually escape cutting or subsequently sprout from the seedbank, thereby negating the effectiveness of mowing as a means for depleting the sources of seed. However, mowing cheatgrass when it exceeds 10 inches in height has been effective at reducing competition from cheatgrass and releasing native grass seedlings in restoration plantings.

Potential Treatments

Biocontrols: Two biocontrols show some promise in controlling cheatgrass and, perhaps, other annual weedy grasses. This work is still preliminary but may offer options in the future, particularly in combination with other treatment methods such as herbicides.

(1) Work by Beckstead, Meyer, and Allen (2011) on the "fungal black fingers of death" (*Pyrenophora semeniperda*) suggests that this fungal pathogen may be useful as a future means for controlling cheatgrass in some areas. Tests suggest that it can kill nearly all of the seeds in target populations, with virtually no risk to nontarget species.

(2) Studies by Kennedy et al. (2011) suggest that a strain of *Pseudomonas fluorescens* bacteria (strain D7) may significantly reduce growth of cheatgrass, medusahead, California brome, and jointed goatgrass, with little effect on other species. Preliminary studies suggest effects may persist for several years after application.

Grazing: Use of livestock to control invasive species has been proposed in various settings, using cattle, sheep, or goats to preferentially reduce or remove various undesirable species. We were unable to find examples of this practice in shrub-steppe restoration in Washington, although some literature suggests possible applications for several species of concern. Several studies have suggested that cheatgrass may be controlled using sheep grazing (Vallentine and Stevens 1994; Miller, Svejcar, and West 1994; Mosley 1996). More recent simulated clipping experiments (Hempy-Mayer and Pyke 2008) provided little support but suggested that combined treatments (e.g., integrating grazing with herbiciding and burning) might produce more acceptable levels of control. Far more experience is needed to determine how the many variables—season, intensity, species and breed of livestock, species and level of weed infestation, etc.—may affect the success of this potential weed control tool.

Broadleaf Weeds

Few weeds rival cheatgrass in their ability to dramatically alter the entire shrub-steppe landscape. However, many broadleaf weeds can become common in degraded Wyoming big sagebrush habitat. Some of the more frequent include tumblemustard, diffuse and spotted knapweed, Dalmatian toadflax, and whitetop.

Moderate-Likelihood Treatments

Integrated approaches: Broadleaf weed infestations in Washington often involve species that lend themselves to integrated, multipronged approaches including biocontrols, manual control, spot herbicide applications, and perhaps grazing. Several biocontrols are available for both knapweeds and toadflax and have shown to be variably effective in Washington (Skillestad 2011). Herbicides frequently used to control such infestations include picloram and 2,4-D, sometimes in combination with glyphosate (Jacobs, Carpinelli, and Sheley 1999; Pokorny and Mangold 2009). Picloram is effective for controlling many broadleaf weeds but can only be used where native forbs are absent or acceptable to remove (Rice et al. 1997; Sheley et al. 2000; Ortega and Pearson 2010, 2011). Residual effects may persist for some time with picloram and some herbicide combinations containing picloram, precluding immediate sowing of native broadleaf seed.

Where single-pass treatments that combine herbiciding and sowing are preferred, nonresidual herbicides are the only solution (e.g., glyphosate, 2,4-D) (Jacobs, Carpinelli, and Sheley 1999).

Low-Likelihood Treatments

Grazing: Various livestock have been used to reduce broadleaf weed infestations in rangelands (DiTomaso 2000; Sheley, Jacobs, and Martin 2004; Rinella and Hileman 2009). However, Rinella and Hileman (2009) note how disparate and even opposite responses can result, depending on numerous interacting factors of timing, species, intensity, and other grazing management practices. As noted previously for annual grasses, we have not encountered significant use of this approach in shrub-steppe restoration in Washington. Although grazing alone may offer only limited promise as a broadleaf weed control strategy, based on some successes in other regions with some species, there appears to be potential for reducing selected weeds while enhancing other desirable species using a well-thought-out integrated pest management program that combines strategic grazing with other techniques.

6.7.4 Increasing Native Species Where Shrubs are Absent

This section examines treatments for enhancing degraded shrub-steppe where shrubs are largely absent (e.g., having been removed by previous fires, treatments, or other factors) and where invasive nonnative species have been largely controlled (Starting States IV, V, and VI from Figure 4, after weed control). Sites in this condition may resemble, in many respects, full field restoration scenarios that have been partially restored. Both situations contend with a matrix of extant, desirable herbaceous species, in which additional species are to be installed to enhance the overall diversity, density, cover, and/or structural complexity of the vegetation. While there is little experience yet with these types of scenarios in degraded shrub-steppe, enhancements of existing full field plantings are being tried in several contexts. Diversification enhancements of Conservation Reserve Program plantings, particularly crested wheatgrass fields, with assistance from Natural Resources Conservation Service programs, offer some insights into alternatives for accomplishing similar objectives in degraded shrub-steppe that we draw upon in this section (Asher and Cotton 2011; Benson 2011).

Planting nursery-grown plugs, rather than direct seeding, may be a preferred approach for species that germinate poorly, where quantities of seed may be extremely limited, and where the soil disturbance necessary to plant seed may be undesirable. However, the growout and planting of plugs, bareroot stock, or other plant parts is expensive, so seeding is generally preferable for diversification of most species. Even so, it is important to employ techniques that deliver appropriate quantities of seed from each species to suitable safe sites in the soil, with the fewest possible number of entries into a site.

Establishing Shrubs

Several unique aspects regarding shrubs and their establishment in restorations deserve consideration separately from other species. Because of the importance of mature big sagebrush plants as key structural and forage elements, many managers have focused on quickly establishing this species, especially where the goal is sage-grouse habitat restoration (Pyke 2011). Planting nursery-grown bareroot stock or tubelings (plugs) has proven successful in many sites (NRCS 1999). In Washington, survival after 7 years was 30-60% with various outplantings (Dettweiler-Robinson et al. 2011; Newsome 2011). Plants generally mature and become reproductive in only a few years, considerably faster than if sown by seed. Because of the relatively high cost of producing and outplanting plants, this approach usually is used to create islands of sagebrush on a site, with the expectation that they will expand through self-seeding (NRCS 1999).

Using seed to establish big sagebrush is slower to produce mature shrubs, and success is more uncertain. Seed may be deliberately sown on a restoration site, naturally dispersed from adults in planted islands (Longland and Bateman 2002; Newsome 2011), or dispersed in from the surrounding shrub-steppe. Shrub seeds are very small and germinate better when sown on the soil surface (e.g., broadcast rather than drill seeded). Seed production is somewhat sporadic and highly dependent on annual moisture, but seeds can be produced in very large quantities (up to 500,000/plant). Within 1 meter of the plant canopy, 85-90% of the seeds fall (Monsen 2011), and the maximum dispersal distance is reported to be 30 meters (Kitchen and Durant McArthur 2007). Monsen (2011) is an excellent source of recent information on restoring big sagebrush from seed. He notes that big sagebrush can recruit native stands of perennial bunchgrasses, but we have observed that the rate and extent of this varies widely in Washington. It appears to be most successful in northern Douglas County (Smith, Benson, personal communication – Appendix 1) and can be very slow and spotty on sites where competition from other species is high and/or seed sources are distant (NRCS 1999).

High-Likelihood Treatments

No-till drill seeding: Delivering each species of seed to the depth most suited for germination reduces many sources of seed loss and failure to establish (Sheley et al. 2008; Asher and Cotton 2011). Drill seeders are the most precise method for accomplishing this. When enhancing rangeland, managers typically seek to restore a mix of grass, forb, and shrub by using seed of different sizes and textures, and only recently has equipment been developed that can handle multiple seed mixes and plant them at different depths on a single pass. Seeding problems can be further compounded in a rangeland setting where the ground is left untilled, and the presence of rocks, rough ground, and surface debris can damage and clog regular cropland seed drills. A new generation of extra heavy duty no-till drills has made it feasible to seed diverse native species into these difficult conditions (*http://www.truaxcomp.com/rangeland.html*). Not only is this equipment designed to plant diverse types of grass and forb seed into the soil at precise depths, but it can also broadcast seeds of shrubs and other species that may be best sown on the ground surface. This equipment ensures good soil/seed contact with the use of imprinters that press the seed firmly onto the soil. These implements are now widely used by the U.S. Forest Service and other agencies (Wiedemann 2007).

Moderate-Likelihood Treatments

Broadcast seeding: Where rangeland drills are unavailable or cannot be used, broadcast seeding is an alternative. Because this approach simply drops the seed on the soil surface, much of the seed fails to work its way into safe sites, leaving it susceptible to predation by rodents and birds, leaving it in positions where it is unable to obtain sufficient moisture or suitable conditions to germinate and survive, or where it may be slow to germinate and therefore compete poorly with other species. Therefore, as a general rule, sown seed densities should be increased by at least 50% over drilled seed application rates (Wiedemann 2007); others recommend increasing rates by a factor of 2-3 times, especially if seedbeds are not prepared (Sheley et al. 2008). Seed can be broadcast manually, using tractors, all-terrain vehicles, or even helicopters. As with herbicide applications, ground-based methods usually are somewhat more effective.

(1) **Broadcast seeding with seedbed preparation and/or followup treatment:** Various devices can be used to put broadcast seed into safe sites, including imprinters, packers, harrows, chain drags, etc. All require, at the very least, an all-terrain vehicle, if not a tractor, to move them across a site and so are limited to sites accessible to such equipment. These treatments can increase germination rates (Lysne 2005;

Sheley et al. 2008), thereby reducing seed costs, but may require a second or even a third entry if the operations cannot be combined. A potential alternative that is occasionally suggested is the use of grazing animals to assist with seed placement through trampling (Pellant and Lysne 2005; Sheley et al. 2008). Hypothetically, if carefully managed, this could be a low-cost means for getting more seed pressed into the soil and more likely to germinate. However, this approach needs to be carefully tested and compared with alternatives; we were unable to find any examples where this approach has been rigorously examined. With all of the implements suggested for imprinting or packing, potentially improved germination of seeded natives must be balanced against the potential of increased disturbance of soil crusts and elevated weed establishment.

(2) **Broadcast seeding of shrubs:** Some shrubs, such as big sagebrush, represent a special case, as their seed is very small and is not suited to drill seeding. Aerial seeding of sagebrush is often attempted, especially in postfire revegetation efforts. However, aerial seeding often results in little or no recruitment. Some greater success has been realized where followup treatments, such as those suggested in "broadcast seeding with seedbed preparation and/or followup treatment," have been applied to achieve greater seed/soil contact (Lysne 2005). The timing of sowing also appears to be critical. Sowing in fall just before winter snowfall is recommended by some, whereas others have found sowing in late winter and even onto snow can be successful (e.g, postfire on Rattlesnake Mountain in Benton County, Washington (Bracken, personal communication – Appendix 1)).

Partial seeding: Striking the right balance between costly, effective treatments and less expensive, ineffective (and ultimately futile) efforts is challenging.

The goal is to sow enough native seeds per unit area to ensure sufficient numbers germinate quickly so as to outcompete competitive weeds that otherwise can rapidly reclaim a restoration site. One compromise is to sow seeds into portions of a site, with the expectation that they will reproduce and continue to infill unseeded areas nearby. This would require less seed than sowing across an entire site, but its success rests upon the likelihood of species successfully expanding outwards from seeded locations. Careful consideration of the species composition and successional patterns at a site will help determine whether expansion of planted species is a reasonable expectation. For the two approaches described next, either drilling or broadcasting may be used, depending on limiting factors at the site.

(1) **Strip seeding:** One approach of partial seeding is to seed species in strips. We encountered one example that attempted to follow this approach (e.g., at Wells Dam (Dan Peterson, personal communication – Appendix 1)) in which a bitterbrush/bunchgrass mix had been sown in 8-feet-wide rows adjacent to 16-feet-wide grass/forb rows. Although these had been in place for approximately 25 years, there was little evidence of the shrubs having filled in the intervening spaces.

2) **Restoration islands:** Another variation of partial planting on a site is the creation of patches or "islands," whereby concentrations of one or several species are planted either by seeding or plugging. Such islands by themselves may provide important habitat for wildlife species that can effectively use patchy resources, such as nectar sources for pollinators, cover for wildlife, etc. (Longland and Bateman 2002). Some islands may also provide many other values (see Section 6.7.5).

Island restoration is also frequently recommended as a means for providing concentrated sources of seed that are able to gradually reseed themselves and spread out across a site (Lysne 2005; Benson et al. 2011). Oddly, there seems to be little solid evidence that this expansion actually occurs with many species, and it runs somewhat counter to several principles of successional management and the dynamics between competitive weeds and establishment of native species.

This disconnect between theory, recommendations, and practice suggests that the expectation of gradual expansion outwards of species from restoration islands must be rigorously tested in the field. We have been unable to find much evidence for such testing in the shrub-steppe restoration literature, despite the frequency with which it is recommended. Our anecdotal observations of species expanding from islands into surrounding habitats are mixed. In some cases, sagebrush islands in restoration plantings have remained largely unchanged in size, whereas we have observed them to spread extensively in others. We have observed a few forbs (e.g., yarrow, daisies, lupines) that appear able to often spread into restoration sites from nearby sources, but many other forbs appear to lack this capacity in most situations. Although we have not been able to identify examples where forb islands have been established in shrub-steppe enhancement efforts, they are used in some Conservation Reserve Program diversification efforts (Asher and Cotton 2011; Benson 2011; Benson et al. 2011), and we consider it a reasonable approach to test (see Section 6.7.5). Generally, most native bunchgrasses do not appear to expand readily into almost any other established vegetation.

Plugging and bare root planting: For some species, planting nursery-grown plugs or bare root stock may be an effective method for bypassing the vulnerable seedling stage and rapidly establishing plants. In Washington shrub-steppe, this approach has been most commonly used with big sagebrush. For example, postfire rehabilitation at Hanford Reach National Monument involved outplanting nearly a million tubelings and bare root sagebrush (Newsome 2011). A quarter or fewer of these are likely to survive to reproductive age. There is wide variability between years and between stock type, with little clear indication of one being superior to another (Dettweiler-Robinson et al. 2011). There has been little planting of forb plugs in a restoration context. We are aware of one project in the Duffy Creek area in Washington (Pam Camp, personal communication – Appendix 1) in which some outplanted plugs received irrigation to see if it enhanced survival. Although many of these plants remain alive after 5 years, there is no evidence of them spreading into surrounding habitat. Grasses generally are not restored by plugging shrub-steppe, as they generally are more effectively established from seed.

Low-Likelihood Treatments

Livestock as seed dispersers: Potentially, livestock can be used to disperse seed across a restoration area by mixing seed in with their feed (Archer and Pyke 1991; Jacobs, Carpinelli, and Sheley 1999). Also, livestock can potentially be used to "imprint" seed into the soil to enhance seed/soil contact (Chris Sheridan, personal communication – Appendix 1). As far as we can ascertain, such ideas are largely hypothetical, and there is little documentation in the published literature that evaluates actual field tests.

Potential Treatments

Grazing: Grazing has been suggested as a potential tool for actively restoring degraded rangeland (Papanastasis 2009). However, this proposal has been most strongly advocated for ecosystems that have a long history of ungulate grazing and hence are well-adapted or even dependent upon this type of disturbance to sustain them. Since shrub-steppe in Washington did not evolve under such grazing pressures (Daubenmire 1970; Mack and Thompson 1982), it would seem unlikely that most grazing regimes would encourage the establishment of native species in a restoration context. However, as with any trials of new or poorly tested restoration treatments, exploration of grazing as a restoration tool should be conducted based on reasonable hypotheses of shrub-steppe ecological functions. Any examination of the potential of grazing as a restoration tool should proceed using the principles of managed succession and adaptive management outlined in Section 6.7.1.

Following this approach, for example, one might hypothesize that a carefully designed grazing regime, perhaps in combination with other treatments, could significantly reduce competition with cheatgrass, minimize competition with established bunchgrasses, and increase soil/seed contact with seeded native forbs through trampling. Rigorous testing and observation might confirm portions of this hypothesis and suggest alternative strategies that might result in more effective treatments to achieve desired results.

6.7.5 Increasing Grasses and Forbs Where Shrubs are Present

This section covers sites where large shrubs are an important component of extant shrub-steppe (Starting States II and III from Figure 4). The presence of large shrubs, such as mature Wyoming big sagebrush, on a site can considerably complicate enhancement restoration actions by limiting access to many types of mechanized equipment. In some cases, it may be simpler and more cost effective to entirely remove the shrub component, carry out the enhancement actions, and then restore the shrubs. However, removing the shrubs in itself can be costly, entailing considerable habitat disturbance that may allow weeds to enter the ecosystem, resulting in the loss of structural components that are key to important wildlife and which will take decades to reestablish. Furthermore, there is a possibility that the shrubs will not reestablish easily on the site. For these reasons, there

are many instances in which enhancement of degraded shrub-steppe should occur where shrubs remain an important part of the vegetation.

As noted at the beginning of Section 6, enhancing extant shrub-steppe involves multiple stages, which include reducing shrub density (if necessary), controlling weeds, and establishing and diversifying bunchgrasses and forbs. While there are numerous examples where restoration efforts in extant shrub-steppe have undertaken each of these strategies, we have not found any examples where the last stage—floristic diversification of the herbaceous species—has been attempted in sites with an extensive, intact shrub component. This is ironic, given the large extent of degraded shrub-steppe in this condition and the importance of enhancing the floristic diversity of these depauperate areas. However, it likely is due to the significant logistical challenges posed by extant shrubs on a site. As a result of this lack of experience upon which to base treatment recommendations, we suggest here some potential options that appear most promising, based on inference from somewhat analogous restoration situations and based on likely outcomes hypothesized from our understanding of succession and other ecological processes in Washington shrub-steppe.

Moderate-Likelihood Treatments

Appropriate treatment options in these circumstances will vary greatly, depending on the extent to which shrub distribution and density, soil conditions (e.g., rockiness, intact biotic crusts), and terrain limit the use of various types of seeding equipment. In many cases, we consider the best alternatives will be variations of the partial seeding approaches described in the previous section (6.7.4.). These alternatives may include different types of strip seeding, as well as restoration of species assemblages in patches and habitat islands of various shapes and sizes. Several features of a patch approach to shrub-steppe enhancement make it particularly attractive in difficult settings:

(1) Patches can be adjusted and modified in area and configuration to fit within the limitations of space, accessibility, and terrain imposed by a site. Thus, depending on their size and location, treatments in patches may be accomplished using tractor-drawn equipment or smaller vehicles, such as all-terrain vehicles, that may be able to make their way between shrubs and across rough terrain.

(2) Patch restoration can be highly individualized, with specific prescriptions of seed mix, mode of application, and treatment sequence tailored to be most suited to the characteristics of the soils and current vegetation on the patch. By using this approach, the natural heterogeneity of most sites can be acknowledged, and the application of unnecessary or inappropriate treatments, which may occur when implementing treatments uniformly across an entire site, can be avoided. This approach may also allow the creation of significantly greater overall species and habitat diversity within a restored area, accommodating rare or uncommon species and assemblages that may otherwise be lost or overlooked in a more uniform restoration approach.

(3) Patch restoration within a larger landscape highlights the important role that productive "hot spots" and islands of suitable habitat can play in sustaining many species within a less-than-pristine larger landscape.

(4) By identifying "low hanging fruit"—landscape patches with more tractable problems and that may most readily respond to restoration efforts—rapid progress can be made with the least effort.

(5) By focusing on many smaller, discrete areas, it may be easier to detect and correct problems as they arise, which otherwise might be missed in the management of single, larger areas.

(6) Progress can be more easily maintained by following an approach that is inherently more flexible and able to accommodate changes in available resources, annual weather, and stochastic events.

This approach is supported by ecological theory pertaining to the dynamics of metapopulations and species and habitat diversity, and variations on it have been advocated in diverse ecosystems (King and Hobbs 2006). Longland and Bateman (2002) have suggested this approach for restoring islands of sagebrush within larger landscapes where fires have removed the shrub layer, an idea that also has been supported for sage-grouse habitat restoration by Meinke, Knick, and Pyke (2009).

Low-Likelihood Treatments

Where extant shrubs preclude ground-based seeding and where larger acreages are to be enhanced, aerial seeding may be attempted. As previously noted, such broadcast seeding requires higher seeding rates (and correspondingly greater costs) and is accompanied by an uncomfortably high likelihood that many species will not successfully establish.

6.7.6 Species Selection

The selection of which species to include in shrub-steppe enhancements depends on many factors. Clearly, the species must be appropriate to the defining characteristics of the site itself (e.g., soils, precipitation, etc.). But attention to successional management concepts also reminds us to consider characteristics of the native species and the invasive weeds with which they may be competing—such characteristics as germinability, growth rates, ability to resist reinvasion, and other competitive abilities. Other factors to consider include seed availability and likely future uses of the site.

When making shrub-steppe enhancements, it is widely recommended to use native species and seed derived from sources as local as possible to ensure best adaptation to local conditions (Sheley et al. 2008).

Although we encountered nonnative wheatgrasses, bluegrasses, native cultivars derived from distant sources, and a variety of nonnative forbs frequently planted in Conservation Reserve Program restoration and diversification projects in Washington, this runs directly counter to what has been strongly advocated in the restoration and rangeland literature for many years (Pyke 1994; Jacobs, Carpinelli, and Sheley 1999). Those involved in shrub-steppe restoration efforts in Washington are now frequently struggling with the difficult challenges posed by removing commonly used and highly competitive species such as sheep fescue and crested, tall, and intermediate wheatgrass (Benson et al. 2011).

The use of nonnative species and nonlocal cultivars may be, at least partly, the result of a lack of availability of native seed from local sources, which underscores the importance of prior planning to ensure adequate quantities of appropriate, local material are available. Growers, such as BFI Native Seeds in Moses Lake, are increasingly developing a wide selection of seeds from local sources around eastern Washington. Excellent sources of information related to using seed of native species in restoration, including shrub-steppe in Washington, include the U.S. Forest Service National Seed Laboratory (*http:// www.nsl.fs.fed.us/great_basin_native_plants.html*), Native Plant Network (*http://www.nativeplantnetwork. org/*), and Native Seed Network (*http://www. nativeseednetwork.org/*). A list of species frequently sown in shrub-steppe restorations in Washington is presented in Table 6.

Table 6. Species commonly seeded in Washington shrub-steppe restorations. * = nonnative species. Sources: P = Pellant and Lysne (2005), B = Benson (2011), T = Benson et al. (2011).

Scientific Name	Common Name	Source
Achillea millefolium	western yarrow	P, B
Achnatherum hymenoides	Indian ricegrass	B
Artemisia tridentata	big sagebrush	P
Atriplex canescens	fourwing saltbush	P
Balsamorhiza sagittata	arrowleaf balsamroot	B
Chrysothamnus nauseosus	rubber rabbitbrush	P
Crepis acuminata	tapertip hawksbeard	B
Elymus cinereus	Great Basin wildrye	T
Elymus elymoides	bottlebrush squirreltail	B
Erigeron filifolius	threadleaf fleabane	B
Erigeron pumilus	shaggy fleabane	B
Eriogonum heracleoides	parsnip-flowered buckwheat	B
Eriogonum niveum	snow buckwheat	T
Eriogonum umbellatum	sulfur-flower buckwheat	B
Festuca idahoensis	Idaho fescue	B
Koehleria macrantha	prairie Junegrass	B
Linum perenne	Lewis flax	P, B
Lomatium triternatum	nineleaf biscuitroot	B
Lupinus sericeus	silky lupine	B
Penstemon palmeri	Palmer penstemon	P
Phlox longifolia	longleaf phlox	T
Poa secunda	Sandberg's bluegrass	B
Pseudoroegneria spicata	bluebunch wheatgrass	B
Purshia tridentata	antelope bitterbrush	P
Sphaeralcea ssp.	globemallow	P
Elymus lanceolatus*	thickspike wheatgrass	B
Medicago sativa*	alfalfa	P
Sanguisorba minor*	small burnet	P

Equipment considerations also may influence choice of seeds. Large-seeded species often establish quickly and are easily handled by seeding equipment, but they perform much better if drilled or sown into tilled ground rather than broadcast and left on the soil surface. In contrast, smaller-seeded species may establish better than larger seeds when broadcast onto untilled soil, but they are generally slower to establish and may lose out in competition with weeds that may still be present.

Some types of seed treatments may enhance germination or survival and may be worth exploring. Seed priming, which is often used in horticultural contexts, may cause seeds to germinate more quickly when sown, allowing them to compete more effectively with weeds (Hardegree and Van Vactor 2000). This may be particularly important for forbs, which tend to have much greater dormancy than grasses (Benson 2011). Fungicide treatments may help protect seeds against various pathogens that can result in costly losses of seed (Jacobs, Carpinelli, and Sheley 1999). Innoculation with mycorrhizae, actinomycetes, and nitrogen-fixing bacteria have also been suggested as means for enhancing establishment of native species (Archer 1994).

When choosing seed mixes, also consider potential advantages that can be derived by including species that differ widely in functional traits. Including species with different root growth forms (e.g., fibrous, tap-rooted, shallow, deep), that grow at different times of year, and that occupy significantly different niches (e.g., annuals, perennials, bulbs, subshrubs) may help establish communities that are more resilient and perhaps more weed resistant (Pyke 1994).

In restoration projects, seeding success can be strongly affected by both the season of planting and the sequence in which different species are sown. Fall sowing is often recommended for many species, but winter and spring sowing may be appropriate for others. Understanding when both natives and invasives typically germinate can help determine which season is better for sowing; consultation with local experts is recommended. Sequencing plantings over a period of time is a possible approach if there seems to be considerable disagreement. Recommendations span the entire range of alternatives, from establishing forbs first and overseeding bunchgrasses later (forbs being generally less competitive and therefore difficult to infill later), to establishing bunchgrasses first and forbs later (grasses being better able to outcompete weeds, and, in the absence of native forbs, followup treatments can be made using broadleaf herbicides), to sowing grasses and forbs together (single entries are substantially less expensive and result in less soil disturbance). Experimentation and careful observation of results at many sites is needed to clarify the tradeoffs and advantages of these alternative approaches.

6.7.7 Assessing Treatment Costs

Successful and cost-effective restoration is the goal of most, if not all, projects. Costs can be challenging to estimate, as they are strongly influenced by site conditions. Sites with sandy soils, less than 10 inches of annual precipitation, and a well-established weed population will require greater time and effort than a loamy soil site with 14 inches of annual precipitation and few weeds. Restoration sites adjacent to well-established native vegetation may benefit over the long term by recolonization of natives and therefore require fewer treatments. Wildlife herbivory may be reduced in sites adjacent to native areas, resulting in lower maintenance. Some of these factors can be anticipated and planned for, but others cannot. Variability in yearly precipitation and other unpredictable and uncontrollable factors (e.g., wildfires, trespass grazing) can thwart even the most meticulously planned and executed projects, adding additional time and cost to a project. In this section, we examine cost planning by breaking it down into four main areas: time, labor, materials, and equipment. Additional useful information in this regard is provided in Benson et al. (2011).

Time: Restoration projects are usually multiyear and generally involve numerous tradeoffs in time and effort, which can affect total project costs. As a general rule, greater initial investments in site preparation and native materials result in fewer entries needed for followup maintenance. This is the preferred strategy, as these greater initial efforts, particularly to control weeds, generally increase the likelihood of long-term success. Initial site preparation loosens the soil and removes biomass to improve seed/soil contact and turns over the soil to bury the weed seed bank. Tradeoff in site preparation may allow increased competition from weeds, which may affect the successful establishment of plant materials. If this initial investment is reduced, fewer native plants may germinate; competition from weeds for space, moisture, and nutrients will be greater;

project duration may increase significantly to correct these problems; and the probability of overall success is lessened.

Labor: Labor is usually needed for relatively short durations during the life of a project, but the timing is often crucial and can be somewhat unpredictable. Therefore, the available labor has to be flexible. Missing crucial timeframes, as may be needed for weed control, can doom the success of a project. Using labor that is experienced with the required type of field work will add to the probability of a successful project, just as experienced farmers are more likely to succeed than inexperienced ones.

Materials: This category includes planting materials (e.g., seed, plugs) and herbicides and is an area of the budget in which costs can vary tremendously. Seed of different species varies widely in cost, and decisions regarding the species and quantities to use in a project may be based on ecological attributes, restoration versus rehabilitation goals, and cost. These decisions will strongly affect the project duration and likelihood of success, as well as the overall ecological outcome.

Native materials often, but not always, cost more than nonnatives or cultivars. Generally, native grass seed is slower to establish than some cultivars and introduced species, but once established, they may be more long lived (i.e., more ecologically adapted) and ecologically compatible with community dynamics and successional trajectories, resulting in a community that includes more native plants and animals and functions more closely to its natural counterparts. Some cultivars may serve the desired ecological role in a community, but background information about their ecology and development needs to be closely reviewed.

Cultivars or introduced grass species that are not well adapted to the site may not persist over time (Jerry Benson, personal communication – Appendix 1) and may need to be replaced later on. Others may

significantly alter ecological processes, resulting in outcomes that only approximate desired objectives. The more aggressive cultivars and nonnatives may limit establishment of forbs, shrubs, and other grasses and may require additional disturbance treatments (e.g., herbicide, mechanical, or fire) in order to achieve diversity objectives on a site. Thus, use of these species may add considerably to the length of time needed to restore a site.

Similar acting herbicides can vary tremendously in price but may differ greatly in effectiveness. Before less expensive herbicides are chosen, consideration should be given to how well they will control problem species, whether multiple applications may be necessary, and how they may affect desirable, nontarget species. Consultation with others with direct experience in comparable situations may provide the best guidance in selecting herbicides and choosing the best timing and methods for applying them.

Equipment: Equipment selection can also significantly affect project costs. The right equipment choice is essential for preparing sites appropriately, applying herbicides effectively, and sowing seeds in ways that enhance germination. However, the most effective equipment may not be available or may add considerably to project costs to rent or contract. As with the previously discussed cost factors, decisions regarding tradeoffs of alternative equipment choices will affect both overall cost and likelihood of success. Discussions on machinery choices and use are available in Benson et al. (2011) and Wiedemann (2007).

Restoration Example

The first 2 years of a project to thin dense sagebrush and seed in strips of grasses are shown in Table 7. Establishment of forbs and subsequent followup treatments are not included in this example. Two alternative treatment approaches were explored— aerial application and ground application. However, not all treatment combinations were considered. The derivation of the cost estimates used in Table 7 is shown in Tables 8 and 9. Total costs of each alternative, relative effectiveness of treatment methods, and the amount of field time needed for each method are discussed.

Cost estimate considerations

Sites: In Table 7, cost estimates are made for a 100-acre area. The cost per acre will be lower for larger areas and higher for smaller areas; movement of machinery is the main factor that contributes to the differences. Restoration options for rocky sites, inaccessible sites, and steep slopes are limited to aerial applications.

Materials: Seed estimates assume an application rate of 10 pounds/acre and a cost of $10/pound. Actual seed costs and rates will vary considerably, depending on species used and site considerations.

Equipment: Equipment rental is assumed. Estimates may vary some depending on the vendor and type of implement. Of course, equipment availability will vary as well. For example, some small-scale equipment may not be available to rent.

Time: Treatments were given a score of 0-2 to reflect the relative amount of time of application (administrative time not included). This was done for comparative purposes in the discussion.

Table 7. Comparison of the cost of two methods for reducing dense sagebrush and planting bunchgrasses.

Treatments		Method 1		Method 2	
Step 1.	Herbicide: sagebrush thinning	Aerial herbicide application (fixed-wing aircraft), $23/acre		Ground-based treatment (2 tractors and chain, boom-spray herbicide), $61/acre	
Result		Minimal soil disturbance, more controlled and uniform amount of sagebrush killed, but dead standing sagebrush to remove before seeding		High level of ground disturbance, patchy removal of sagebrush and other species, but seedbed ready to seed	
Effectiveness		High		High	
Logistics		Minimum time – 0		Maximum time – 1	
Step 2.	Seedbed preparation	$50/acre (x2): Removal of biomass and seedbed preparation (2 passes, 2 implements)		$50/acre: Leveling out the seedbed (1 pass, 1 implement)	
Result		High level of ground disturbance, may cause some additional shrub kill		Not much additional ground disturbance	
Effectiveness		High		High	
Logistics		Maximum time (double) – 2		Less time – 1	
Step 3.	Grass seeding	Aerial $212/acre	Ground $150/acre	Aerial $212/acre	Ground $150/acre
Result		Lower soil/seed contact	Best soil/seed contact	Lower soil/seed contact	Best soil/seed contact
Effectiveness		Less effective	More effective	Less effective	More effective
Logistics		Minimum time – 0	Maximum time – 1	Minimum time – 0	Maximum time – 1
Step 4.	Herbicide: weed treatment	Aerial $12.35/acre	Ground $50.35/acre	Aerial $12.35/acre	Ground $50.35/acre
Results		Aerial less effective than ground application		Aerial less effective than ground application	
Effectiveness		Less effective	More effective	Less effective	More effective
Logistics		Minimum time – 0	Maximum time – 1	Minimum time – 0	Maximum time – 1
Summary					
Total treatment cost		$347.35/acre	$323.35/acre	$335.35/acre	$311.35/acre
Effectiveness		Effective removal and prep, less effective seeding	Effective removal and prep, effective seeding	Effective removal and prep, less effective seeding	Effective removal and prep, effective seeding
Logistics time		2*	4	2	4

*See Appendix 3, Section V., for more details on cost estimation derivations.

Table 8. Herbicide, seed, and applicator costs used in Table 7 example.

	Herbicide		Native Seed
	Tebuthiuron $11/acre (sagebrush thinning)	**Postplanting low dose Roundup (4 oz/acre) $.35/acre**	**$200/acre (aerial) (x2)*** **$100/acre (ground)**
Aerial application (fixed-wing aircraft) $12/acre	$23/acre	$12.35/acre	$212/acre
Ground application (tractor) $50/acre	$61/acre	$50.35/acre	$150/acre

*Multiplier factor from Benson et al. (2011).

Table 9. Equipment and labor costs used in Table 7 example.

Ground Application - Mechanical	
1. Equipment rental: tractor ($20/acre) + implement ($15/acre)	$35/acre
2. Field labor: $28/hr field work - 4 acre/hr average	$7/acre
3. Logistics: (move equipment, 2 days, or 16 hrs), ($25 x 2 people x 16 hrs) = $800/100-acre treatment	$8/acre
4 Tebuthiuron (sagebrush thinning)	$11/acre
TOTAL	**$61/acre**

In Table 7, costs per acre range from $311.35/acre to $347.35/acre, with ground application for the entire process the most cost-effective approach in this example. The difference in the cost of grass seeding contributed the largest amount of variance between aerial and ground application costs. All of the numbers used in this example could vary widely, depending on local circumstances, so they should not be applied uncritically. The costs per acre could be reduced a number of ways in this example:

Machine rental versus ownership considerations: Finding the right implement to rent when you need it may prove challenging. Many restoration projects are intermediate in scale, encompassing only a few hundred acres. But the traditional rental market caters either to home gardeners (small scale) or commercial agricultural production (large scale), neither of which may work well on an intermediate scale. Using larger equipment may not be logistically possible, and smaller equipment may double the labor time in use. For larger equipment, there may be move charges as well, which adds further to the cost. Sharing equipment with managers at other restoration sites may be the most cost-effective solution.

Alternatively, at times, it may be most cost effective to purchase some types of equipment. For example, a

15-foot mower may cost $15,000 and is estimated to cost $15/acre to operate. Thus, it would become cost efficient after 1,000 acres. A $50,000 tractor rented at $20/acre would be cost effective after 2,500 acres. A trailer to haul equipment would be necessary in either case. Ownership may help compensate for volatile, yearly budgets, but one should not overlook the cost and expertise required for ongoing maintenance.

Labor and time tradeoff: If labor is in short supply during the critical weed control window of time, contracting for field work is an option. An herbicide applicator may cost $25/hour (labor only). However, if a substantial amount of restoration is anticipated, an in-house crew may be more cost effective or may be more reliably available during the critical times. It cannot be overemphasized that meeting critical windows of time in a restoration project may mean the difference between success and failure.

Other considerations: As noted previously, cost is only one of the factors to be considered in this example. Ground disturbance is certain to be higher with chaining and planting and may be a key consideration in some sites. Availability of time and labor are not factored into this example, although the amount of field labor would vary considerably between the scenarios. Effectiveness of methods may be the most important consideration. Aerial seed applications tend to have a much lower seeding success rate than ground-based applications. Likewise, ground applications tend to control weeds more successfully, although the magnitude of difference in effectiveness is not nearly so wide as with seeding. Cost estimates for weed control are extremely uncertain, as effectiveness can be very difficult to predict. Reinfestations often occur due to inadequate initial control, which can be especially problematic in restoring extant shrub-steppe. If the site is particularly weedy, starting over using approaches for restoring potential shrub-steppe, such as described in Benson et al. (2011) should be considered.

6.7.8 Reconciling Treatments with Transitions

The state-and-transition model in Figure 4 provides a means for more rigorously considering shrub-steppe restoration from a successional management perspective. Understanding how the transitions that link the starting and restored states mesh with restoration treatments and successional pathways is valuable in making decisions about what sites to restore, how to go about accomplishing these habitat enhancements, and the likelihood of these actions being successful. Here, we revisit the previously described transitions (Section 5.4) and consider how they can be related to the treatments described in this section.

The combinations of treatments described in Section 6.7 are the mechanisms that bring about each of the transitions in Figure 4. In Section 6.4, we suggested how transitions might be broken down into several stages or phases. Building on the hypothetical example we illustrated in Figure 6, T1b involves reducing the abundance of big sagebrush, controlling invasive weeds, and increasing native bunchgrasses and forbs as needed. This might be accomplished by (1) aerially spraying Tebuthiuron to reduce sagebrush cover and open the canopy up to allow for (2) a late-winter application of glyphosate to reduce cheatgrass abundance, followed by (3) patch planting of forbs and grasses in select islands among the remaining sagebrush, and (4) a followup late-winter glyphosate application to control remaining cheatgrass.

This type of staged, multientry series of treatments to bring about the transition of a site to a restored state challenges the capabilities of traditional state-and-transition modeling. It is difficult to calculate the probability of different transitions that are comprised of combinations of treatments, each of which is associated with its own, highly uncertain probability. Collectively, this introduces many layers of complexity and potential error. We suggest the following approach as a means for beginning to use these as conceptual tools to aid in restoration planning.

Each of the treatment categories—high, moderate, and low—can be thought of as occupying a probability range associated with the likelihood of success. The "high" category might be in the range of 0.5-0.7, moderate equals 0.3-0.5, and low equals 0.0-0.3. These are just rough guesses, and further tweaking might make them more accurately reflect the real probability of success for each treatment. There are several ways one might combine the probabilities to arrive at an overall figure for a combination of treatments. Multiplying them together (following traditional probability theory) might be the simplest approach to derive a rough number that could be used to compare different treatments.

It is important to recognize, however, that these probabilities—uncertain as they are—only refer to the likelihood of the "complete" success of a treatment (i.e., all sown species surviving in the abundances expected, all weeds controlled to the anticipated levels, etc.). In reality, there are also ranges of success associated with every treatment. Thus, some sown forbs may be complete failures, while others are stunning successes, and still others are somewhere in the middle. Considering treatment success this way, as the sum of their individual components, most treatments probably end up as partial successes. Deciding whether a transition has successfully moved a site to another state then depends on how clearly the state boundaries can be defined and how accurately a site can be characterized, as in one state or another. The answers are important—will a restored site remain in its enhanced condition, or have critical thresholds not been crossed, and will it slide back into its degraded state? However, these are difficult questions that will take time, experimentation, and careful monitoring to answer.

References

Aldridge, C.L., S.E. Nielsen, H.L. Beyer, M.S. Boyce, J.W. Connelly, S.T. Knick, and M.A. Schroeder. 2008. Range-wide patterns of greater sage-grouse persistence. Diversity and Distributions 14 (6): 983-994.

Archer, S. 1994. Woody plant encroachment into southwestern grasslands and savannas: rates, patterns and proximate causes. p. 13-68. In: Vavra, M., W. Laycock, and R.D. Pieper (eds). Ecological implications of livestock herbivory in the West. Society for Range Management, Denver, CO.

Archer, S., and D.A. Pyke. 1991. Plant-animal interactions affecting plant establishment and persistence on revegetated rangeland. Journal of Range Management 44 (6): 558-565.

Asher, M., and J. Cotton. 2011. Inter-seeding Native Forbs and Shrubs into Established Grass Stands. Columbia Basin Landscapes Workshop: Linking Science and Management to Improve Restoration Success in the Shrub Steppe. Friends of Mid-Columbia River Wildlife Refuges, Kennewick, WA.

Baker, W.L. 2006. Fire and Restoration of Sagebrush Ecosystems. Wildlife Society Bulletin 34 (1): 177-185.

Baker, W.L. 2011. Pre-Euro-American and Recent Fire in Sagebrush Ecosystems. p. 185-201. In: Knick, S., and J.W. Connelly (eds). Greater Sage-Grouse: Ecology and Conservation of a Landscape Species and Its Habitats. University of California Press, Berkeley, California.

Baker, W.L., J. Garner, and P. Lyon. 2009. Effect of Imazapic on Cheatgrass and Native Plants in Wyoming Big Sagebrush Restoration for Gunnison Sage-Grouse. Natural Areas Journal 29 (3): 204-209.

Beckstead, J., S. Meyer, and P. Allen. 2011. Field inoculation trials demonstrate that a seed pathogen can eliminate the cheatgrass carryover seed bank. Columbia Basin Landscapes Workshop: Linking Science and Management to Improve Restoration Success in the Shrub Steppe. Friends of Mid-Columbia River Wildlife Refuges, Kennewick, WA.

Belnap, J., and O.L. Lange (eds). 2001. Biological Soil Crusts: Structure, Function, and Management. Springer-Verlag, Berlin, Germany.

Belnap, J., R. Rosentreter, S. Leonard, J.H. Kaltenecker, J. Williams, and D. Eldridge. 2001. Biological Soil Crusts: Ecology and Management. Tech Ref 1730-2. Bureau of Land Management, National Science and Technology Center, Denver, CO.

Benson, J.E. 2011. Crested Wheatgrass Diversification: Practical Experiences. Columbia Basin Landscapes Workshop: Linking Science and Management to Improve Restoration Success in the Shrub Steppe. Friends of Mid-Columbia River Wildlife Refuges, Kennewick, WA.

Benson, J.E., R.T. Tveten, M.G. Asher, and P.W. Dunwiddie. 2011. Shrub-Steppe and Grassland Restoration Manual for the Columbia River Basin. Washington Department of Fish and Wildlife, Olympia, WA. http://wdfw.wa.gov/publications/01330/wdfw01330.pdf.

Bestelmeyer, B.T. 2006. Threshold Concepts and Their Use in Rangeland Management and Restoration: The Good, the Bad, and the Insidious. Restoration Ecology 14 (3): 325-329.

Bestelmeyer, B.T., A.J. Tugel, G.L. Peacock, D.G. Robinett, P.L. Shaver, J.R. Brown, J.E. Herrick, H. Sanchez, and K.M. Havstad. 2009. State-and-Transition Models for Heterogeneous Landscapes: A Strategy for Development and Application. Rangeland Ecology and Management 62 (1): 1-15.

Blumenthal, D.M., U. Norton, J.D. Derner, and J.D. Reeder. 2006. Long-term effects of tebuthiuron on *Bromus tectorum*. Western North American Naturalist 66 (4): 420-425.

Booth, M.S., J.M. Stark, and M.M. Caldwell. 2003. Inorganic N turnover and availability in annual- and perennial-dominated soils in a northern Utah shrub-steppe ecosystem. Biogeochemistry 66: 311-330.

Boyd, C.S., and T.J. Svejcar. 2009. Managing Complex Problems in Rangeland Ecosystems. Rangeland Ecology and Management 62 (6): 491-499.

Briske, D.D., B.T. Bestelmeyer, T.K. Stringham, and P.L. Shaver. 2008. Recommendations for Development of Resilience-Based State-and-Transition Models. Rangeland Ecology and Management 61 (4): 359-367.

Briske, D.D., S.D. Fuhlendorf, and F.E. Smeins. 2003. Vegetation dynamics on rangelands: a critique of the current paradigms. Journal of Applied Ecology 40: 601-614.

Briske, D.D., S.D. Fuhlendorf, and F.E. Smeins. 2005. State-and-Transition Models, Thresholds, and Rangeland Health: A Synthesis of Ecological Concepts and Perspectives. Rangeland Ecology and Management 58: 1-10.

Clary, W.P., S. Goodrich, and B.M. Smith. 1985. Response to Tebuthiuron by Utah Juniper and Mountain Big Sagebrush Communities. Journal of Range Management 38 (1): 56-60.

Clewell, A., J. Rieger, and J. Munro. 2005. Guidelines for Developing and Managing Ecological Restoration Projects. Society for Ecological Restoration International.

Connelly, J.W., E.T. Rinkes, and C.E. Braun. 2011. Characteristics of Greater Sage-Grouse Habitats: A Landscape Species at Micro- and Macroscales. p. 69-83. In: Knick, S.T., and J.W. Connelly (eds). Greater Sage-Grouse: Ecology and Conservation of a Landscape Species and Its Habitats. University of California Press, Berkeley, CA.

Cox, R.D., and V.J. Anderson. 2004. Increasing native diversity of cheatgrass-dominated rangeland through assisted succession. Rangeland Ecology and Management 57 (2): 203-210.

Dahlgren, D.K., R. Chi, and T.A. Messmer. 2006. Greater Sage-Grouse Response to Sagebrush Management in Utah. Wildlife Society Bulletin 34 (4): 975-985.

Daubenmire, R.F. 1970. Steppe Vegetation of Washington. Tech Bulletin 62. Washington Agricultural Experiment Station.

Davies, G.M., J.D. Bakker, E. Dettweiler-Robinson, P.W. Dunwiddie, S.A. Hall, J. Downs, and J. Evans. 2012. Trajectories of change in sagebrush steppe vegetation communities in relation to multiple wildfires. Ecological Applications 22 (5): 1562-1577.

Davies, K.W., J.D. Bates, D.D. Johnson, and A.M. Nafus. 2009. Influence of Mowing *Artemisia tridentata* ssp. *wyomingensis* on Winter Habitat for Wildlife. Environmental Management 44: 84-92.

Davies, K.W., and R.L. Sheley. 2011. Promoting Native Vegetation and Diversity in Exotic Annual Grass Infestations. Restoration Ecology 19 (2): 159-165.

Davison, J.C., and E.G. Smith. 2007. Imazapic provides 2-year control of weedy annuals in a seeded Great Basin fuelbreak. Native Plants Journal 8 (2): 91-95.

Dettweiler-Robinson, E., J.R. Evans, H. Newsome, R. Haugo, G.M. Davies, J.D. Bakker, P.W. Dunwiddie, D. Pyke, and T. Wirth. 2011. Restoring Wyoming big sagebrush following wildfire using nursery-grown stock: Contrasting methods and predicting survival. Society for Ecological Restoration, Austin, TX.

DiTomaso, J.M. 2000. Invasive weeds in rangelands: Species, impacts, and management. Weed Science 48 (2): 255-265.

Elzinga, C.L., D.W. Salzer, and J.W. Willoughby. 1998. Measuring & Monitoring Plant Populations. Tech Ref 1730-1. Bureau of Land Management, National Applied Resource Sciences Center, Denver, CO.

Evans, J.R., and M.P. Lih. 2005. Recovery and Rehabilitation of Vegetation on the Fitzner-Eberhardt Arid Lands Ecology Reserve, Hanford Reach National Monument, Following the 24 Command Fire. The Nature Conservancy, Seattle, WA.

Evans, R.D., and J. Belnap. 1999. Long-Term Consequences of Disturbance on Nitrogen Dynamics in an Arid Ecosystem. Ecology 80 (1): 150-160.

Hardegree, S.P., and S.S. Van Vactor. 2000. Germination and Emergence of Primed Grass Seeds Under Field and Simulated-field Temperature Regimes. Annals of Botany 85 (3): 379-390.

Hays, D.W., M.J. Tirhi, and D.W. Stinson. 1998. Washington State Status Report for the Sage Grouse. Washington Department of Fish and Wildlife, Olympia, WA.

Hempy-Mayer, K., and D.A. Pyke. 2008. Defoliation Effects on *Bromus tectorum* Seed Production: Implications for Grazing. Rangeland Ecology and Management 61 (1): 116-123.

Hemstrom, M.A., M.J. Wisdom, W.J. Hann, M.M. Rowland, B.C. Wales, and R.A. Gravenmier. 2002. Sagebrush-steppe vegetation dynamics and restoration potential in the interior Columbia Basin, USA. Conservation Biology 16 (5): 1243-1255.

Jacobs, J.S., M.F. Carpinelli, and R.L. Sheley. 1999. Revegetating Noxious Weed-Infested Rangeland. p. 133-141. In: Sheley, R.L., and J.K. Petroff (eds). Review of Biology and Management of Noxious Rangeland Weeds. Oregon State University Press, Corvallis, OR.

Johnson, W.M. 1958. Reinvasion of Big Sagebrush Following Chemical Control. Journal of Range Management 11: 169-172.

Kennedy, A.C., T.L. Stubbs, J.C. Hansen, and R. Schultheis. 2011. Biological Control Using Soil Microorganisms. U.S. Department of Agriculture and Washington State University.

King, E.G., and R.J. Hobbs. 2006. Identifying Linkages Among Conceptual Models of Ecosystem Degradation and Restoration: Towards an Integrative Framework. Restoration Ecology 14 (3): 369-378.

Kitchen, S.G., and E. Durant McArthur. 2007. Big and Black Sagebrush Landscapes. p. 73-95. In: Hood, S.M., and M. Miller (eds). Fire Ecology and Management of the Major Ecosystems of Southern Utah. Gen Tech Rep RMRS-GTR-202. U.S. Forest Service, Rocky Mountain Research Station, Fort Collins, CO.

Knick, S.T., and J.W. Connelly (eds). 2011. Greater Sage-Grouse: Ecology and Conservation of a Landscape Species and Its Habitats. University of California Press, Berkeley, CA.

Krueger-Mangold, J.M., R.L. Sheley, and T.J. Svejcar. 2006. Toward ecologically-based invasive plant management on rangeland. Weed Science 54 (3): 597-605.

Laycock, W.A. 1991. Stable states and thresholds of range condition on North American rangelands: A viewpoint. Journal of Range Management 44 (5): 427-433.

Link, S.O., and R.W. Hill. 2011. Management of fuel loading in the shrub-steppe: Responses six and seven years after treatments. Columbia Basin Landscapes Workshop: Linking Science and Management to Improve Restoration Success in the Shrub Steppe. Friends of the Mid-Columbia River Wildlife Refuges, Kennewick, WA.

Link, S.O., W.H. Mast, R.W. Hill, and M.L. Pellant. 2004. Restoration Encyclopedia: Shrub-Steppe Restoration. In: Proceedings of the 16th International Conference, Society for Ecological Restoration, Victoria, BC.

Longland, W.S., and S.L. Bateman. 2002. Viewpoint: The ecological value of shrub islands on disturbed sagebrush rangelands. Journal of Range Management 55: 571-575.

Lysne, C.R. 2005. Restoring Wyoming Big Sagebrush. U.S. Forest Service, Rocky Mountain Research Station, Fort Collins, CO.

Mack, R.N., and J.N. Thompson. 1982. Evolution in Steppe with Few Large, Hooved Mammals. The American Naturalist 119 (6): 757-773.

McCune, B. 2007. Improved estimates of incident radiation and heat load using non-parametric regression against topographic variables. Journal of Vegetation Science 18 (5): 751-754.

McIver, J., M. Brunson, S. Bunting, J. Chambers, N. Devoe, P. Doescher, J. Grace, D. Johnson, S. Knick, R. Miller, M. Pellant, and others. 2010. The Sagebrush Steppe Treatment Evaluation Project (SageSTEP): A Test of State-and-Transition Theory. Gen Tech Rep RMRS-GTR-237. U.S. Forest Service, Rocky Mountain Research Station, Fort Collins, CO.

Meinke, C.W., S.T. Knick., and D.A. Pyke. 2009. A Spatial Model to Prioritize Sagebrush Landscapes in the Intermountain West (U.S.A.) for Restoration. Restoration Ecology 17 (5): 652-659.

Mensing, S., S. Livingston, and P. Barker. 2006. Long-term fire history in Great Basin sagebrush reconstructed from macroscopic charcoal in spring sediments, Newark Valley, Nevada. Western North American Naturalist 66 (1): 64-77.

Miller, R.F., T.J. Svejcar, and N.E. West. 1994. Implications of livestock grazing in the intermountain sagebrush region: plant composition. p. 101-46. In: Vavra, M., W.A. Laycock, and R.D. Pieper (eds). Ecological implications of livestock herbivory in the West. Society for Range Management, Denver, CO.

Miller, R.F., S.T. Knick, D.A. Pyke, C.W. Meinke, S.E. Hanser, M.J. Wisdom, and A.L. Hild. 2011. Characteristics of Sagebrush Habitats and Limitations to Long-Term Conservation. p. 145-184. In: Knick, S.T., and J.W. Connelly (eds). Greater Sage-Grouse: Ecology and Conservation of a Landscape Species and Its Habitats. University of California Press, Berkeley, CA.

Monsen, S.B., 2011. Biological and Ecological Aspects of Big Sagebrush Subspecies: Influences on Planting Success and Community Restoration. Wyoming Shrub Reestablishment Workshop. Wyoming Reclamation and Restoration Center, University of Wyoming.

Mosley, J.C. 1996. Prescribed sheep grazing to suppress Cheatgrass: a review. Sheep and Goat Research Journal 12: 74-80.

Newsome, H. 2011. Planting seedlings to regenerate critical shrub components in shrub-steppe; a viable tool for land managers. Columbia Basin Landscapes Workshop: Linking Science and Management to Improve Restoration Success in the Shrub Steppe. Friends of Mid-Columbia River Wildlife Refuges, Kennewick, WA.

NRCS (Natural Resources Conservation Service). 1999. Restoration of Woody Plants within Native Range Communities. Plant Materials Tech Note MT-31. U.S. Department of Agriculture, Montana.

Olson, R.A., J. Hansen, and T.D. Whitson. 1996. Enhancing rangeland forage production and biodiversity with tebuthiuron. Sharing Common Ground on Western Rangelands: Proceedings of a Livestock/Big Game Symposium. Gen Tech Rep INT-GTR-343. U.S. Forest Service, Intermountain Research Station.

Ortega, Y.K., and D.E. Pearson. 2010. Effects of picloram application on community dominants vary with initial levels of spotted knapweed (*Centaurea stoebe*) invasion. Invasive Plant Science and Management 3: 70-80.

Ortega, Y.K., and D.E. Pearson. 2011. Long-term effects of weed control with picloram along a gradient of spotted knapweed invasion. Rangeland Ecology and Management 64: 67-77.

Papanastasis, V.P. 2009. Restoration of Degraded Grazing Lands through Grazing Management: Can It Work? Restoration Ecology 17 (4): 441-445.

Pellant, M., J. Kaltenecker, and S. Jirik. 1999. Use of OUST® Herbicide to Control Cheatgrass in the Northern Great Basin. USDA Forest Service Proceedings RMRS-P-9. U.S. Forest Service, Rocky Mountain Research Station.

Pellant, M., and C.R. Lysne. 2005. Strategies to Enhance Plant Structure and Diversity in Crested Wheatgrass Seedings. p. 81-92. In: Shaw, N.L., M. Pellant, and S.B. Monsen (comps). Sage-Grouse Habitat Restoration Symposium Proceedings. RMRS-P-38. U.S. Forest Service, Rocky Mountain Research Station, Fort Collins, CO.

Pokorny, M.L., and J.M. Mangold. 2009. Converting Pasture Land to Native-Plant-Dominated Grassland: A Case Study (Montana). Ecological Restoration 27 (3): 250-253.

Ponzetti, J.M., B. McCune, and D.A. Pyke. 2007. Biotic soil crusts in relation to topography, cheatgrass and fire in the Columbia Basin, Washington. The Bryologist 110 (4): 706-722.

Pyke, D.A. 1994. Rangeland Seedings and Plantings: Exotics or Natives? In: Sustaining Rangeland Ecosystems Symposium, La Grande, OR.

Pyke, D.A. 2011. Restoring and Rehabilitating Sagebrush Habitats. p. 531-548. In: Knick, S.T., and J.W. Connelly (eds). Greater Sage-Grouse: Ecology and Conservation of a Landscape Species and Its Habitats. University of California Press, Berkeley, CA.

Pyke, D.A., M.D. Reisner, P.S. Doescher, E.W. Schupp, J. Chambers, J. Grace, S. Shaff, J. Burnham, and A. Lindgren. 2011. Fuel Treatments, Livestock Grazing, and Invasibility – Some Preliminary Results from SageSTEP. Columbia Basin Landscapes Workshop: Linking Science and Management to Improve Restoration Success in the Shrub Steppe. Friends of Mid-Columbia River Wildlife Refuges, Kennewick, WA.

Rafferty, D.L., and J.A. Young. 2002. Cheatgrass competition and establishment of desert needlegrass seedlings. Journal of Range Management 55: 70-72.

Reever Morghan, K.J., R.L. Sheley, and T.J. Svejcar. 2006. Successful Adaptive Management—The Integration of Research and Management. Rangeland Ecology and Management 59 (2): 216-219.

Rice, P.M., J.C. Toney, D.J. Bedunah, and C.E. Carlson. 1997. Plant community diversity and growth form responses to herbicide applications for control of *Centaurea maculosa*. Journal of Applied Ecology 34: 1397-1412.

Ridenour, W.M., and R.M. Callaway. 2001. The relative importance of allelopathy in interference: the effects of an invasive weed on a native bunchgrass. Oecologia 126: 444-450.

Rinella, M.J., and B.J. Hileman. 2009. Efficacy of prescribed grazing depends on timing intensity and frequency. Journal of Applied Ecology 46: 796-803.

SageSTEP. 2010. Plateau Pre-Emergent Herbicide Suppresses Invasive Exotics Following Fuels Treatments. p. 1-3. In: SageSTEP News, Issue 13.

SER (Society for Ecological Restoration International Science and Policy Working Group). 2004. SER International Primer on Ecological Restoration. Society for Ecological Restoration International, Tucson, AZ.

Sheley, R.L., C.A. Duncan, M.B. Halstvedt, and J.S. Jacobs. 2000. Spotted knapweed and grass response to herbicide treatments. Journal of Range Management 53 (2): 176-182.

Sheley, R.L., J.S. Jacobs, and J.M. Martin. 2004. Integrating 2,4-D and sheep grazing to rehabilitate spotted knapweed infestations. Rangeland Ecology and Management 57 (4): 371-375.

Sheley, R., J. James, B. Smith, and E. Vasquez. 2010. Applying Ecologically Based Invasive-Plant Management. Rangeland Ecology and Management 63 (6): 605-613.

Sheley, R., J. Mangold, K. Goodwin, and J. Marks. 2008. Revegetation Guidelines for the Great Basin: Considering Invasive Weeds. ARS-168. U.S. Department of Agriculture, Agricultural Research Service, Washington, DC.

Skillestad, L. 2011. Insects with an Attitude: Biocontrol Agents for Noxious Weeds. Columbia Basin Landscapes Workshop: Linking Science and Management to Improve Restoration Success in Shrub Steppe. Friends of the Columbia Basin Wildlife Refuge, Kennewick, WA.

Sperry, L.J., J. Belnap, and R.D. Evans. 2006. *Bromus tectorum* invasion alters nitrogen dynamics in an undisturbed arid grassland ecosystem. Ecology 87 (3): 603-615.

Stevens, R., and S.B. Monsen. 2004. Mechanical Plant Control. p. 65-88. In: Monsen, S.B., R. Stevens, N.L. Shaw (comps). Restoring Western Ranges and Wildlands. Vol 1, Gen Tech Rep RMRS-GTR-136. U.S. Forest Service Rocky Mountain Research Station, Fort Collins, CO.

Vallentine, J.F., and A.R. Stevens. 1994. Use of livestock to control cheatgrass—a review. p. 202-206. In: Monsen, S.B., and S.G. Kitchen (compilers). Proceedings—ecology and management of annual rangelands. Gen Tech Rep INT-GTR-313. U.S. Forest Service, Intermountain Research Station, Boise, ID.

Westoby, M., B. Walker, and I. Noy-Meir. 1989. Opportunistic management for rangelands not at equilibrium. Journal of Range Management 42 (4): 266-274.

Wiedemann, H. 2007. Revegetation Equipment Catalog. U.S. Forest Service, Bureau of Land Management, Rangeland Technology and Equipment Council.

Wirth, T.A., and D.A. Pyke. 2007. Monitoring Post-Fire Vegetation Rehabilitation Projects: A Common Approach for Non-Forested Ecosystems. Special Investigations Report 2006-5048. U.S. Geological Survey, Reston, VA.

Appendix 1. List of Practitioners Contacted Regarding Shrub-Steppe Restoration

Name	Agency
Mel Asher	BFI Native Seeds
Jerry Benson	Private
Molly Boyter	Bureau of Land Management
Ed Bracken	Private
Pam Camp	formerly with Bureau of Land Management
Cindi Confer	Washington Department of Fish and Wildlife
Janelle Downs	Pacific Northwest National Laboratory
Richard Easterly	Private
Mike Finch	Washington Department of Fish and Wildlife
Richard Fleenor	Natural Resources Conservation Service
Sonia Hall	The Nature Conservancy
Marc Hallet	Washington Department of Fish and Wildlife
Neal Hedges	Chelan-Douglas Land Trust
Colin Leingang	Yakima Training Center
Steve Link	Private
Pete Lopushinsky	Washington Department of Fish and Wildlife
Heidi Newsome	U.S. Fish and Wildlife Service
Jim Olson	Washington Department of Fish and Wildlife
Mike Pellant	Bureau of Land Management
Dan Peterson	Washington Department of Fish and Wildlife
David Pyke	U.S. Geological Survey
Roger Rosentreter	Bureau of Land Management
Rocky Ross	formerly with Washington Department of Fish and Wildlife
Jerry Rouse	Natural Resources Conservation Service
Debra Salstrom	Private
Mike Schroeder	Washington Department of Fish and Wildlife
Chris Sheridan	Bureau of Land Management
Courtney Smith	Natural Resources Conservation Service
Mark Stannard	Natural Resources Conservation Service
David St. George	The Nature Conservancy
Katrina Strathmann	Yakama Nation
Richard Tveten	Washington Department of Fish and Wildlife
Chuck Warner	The Nature Conservancy
Berta Youtie	Private

Appendix 2. Restoration Project Documentation Form

(Benson et al. 2011)

Delete instructions (gray font) as form is completed.

Recorded by:

Contact information:

Date recorded:

Location and site attributes:

Project Name			
County			
Location	T R S	Lat.	Long.
Wildlife Area and Unit			
Restored Area Size			
Ownership			
Elevation	*Useful link http://www.earthtools.org/*		
Aspect			
Slope			
Annual Precipitation	*Useful link http://prismmap.nacse.org/nn/index.phtml*		

Soils: *Provide a brief description of the major soil types on the site. This may include populating Table 1, which is attached.*

Adjacent land use and condition: *Describe uses that may impact the project site (e.g., native species, weed infestations, fire risk, herbicide use, grazing, farmland).*

Site history: *Describe former land use (e.g., Conservation Reserve Program, grazing, other) and prerestoration dominant species composition.*

Project goals: *Explain what you hope to achieve (short and long term). Include cover and composition goals if they were defined. (Table 1 may be helpful when setting vegetation goals.)*

Site preparation: *Summarize specific site preparation measures and the sequence in which they were carried out in Table 2. Include any overall site preparation comments here (see Table 2, attached).*

Seed mix: *List the species used, and provide copies of the tags (see Table 3, attached).*

Planting: *Provide details of planting methods in Table 4, attached.*

Postplanting weed control and other management actions: *See Table 5, attached.*

Evaluation of Current Conditions

As restoration site conditions vary over time, it is advisable to periodically assess site status. New copies of this section can be completed and attached each time a new assessment is made.

Date of status assessment: _____

Current status: *Describe the current status of planted species and weeds. Summarize weed control effectiveness.*

Goals realization: *How close are you to what you intended to restore? Relate original goals to current status.*

Special circumstances affecting outcomes: *Note postrestoration events, such as extreme weather, fires, disease problems, etc., as well as good things like native species re-invasion.*

Keys to present level of success: *Note special actions or circumstances that may have improved project outcomes and lessons that have been learned. What would you have done differently?*

Project site future: *What do you plan to do, or what would you like to do to make further improvements?*

Table 1: Soils, Ecological Sites or Reference Sites, and Presumed Dominant Species.

*Information can be summarized in the following table. Sample data often may be derived from the following two websites. The web soil survey link can be used to provide site-specific information on potential vegetation and can be accessed at **http://websoilsurvey.nrcs.usda.gov/app/WebSoilSurvey.aspx**. Once a specific "Area of Interest" has been designated using the AOI tab, navigate using the "Soil Data Explorer" tab or the "Ecological Site Assessment" tab, where you can find the ecological site description; these can also be found in the custom soils report. Another website that can be used to download ecological site descriptions is **http://efotg.sc.egov.usda.gov/efotg_locator.aspx?map=WA**. Once at this site, select the county of interest, select section II in the drop down box on left side of the screen, and then open the "Ecological Site Descriptions" folder at the bottom of the folder list. Attach the reports as attachments B1, B2,…B# for those who may wish to study them further or compare goals to predegradation conditions.*

While ecological site descriptions are often a convenient way to learn about historical conditions, such descriptions are not always available or may contradict other available sources. As an alternative, or in addition to the aforementioned websites, information on potential native plant species may be compiled by examining less-disturbed nearby sites, if they exist, or other references.

Soils	% of Site	Ecological Site Name or Reference Site Description	Presumed Dominant Species Composition in Healthy Condition

Table 2: Site Preparation. *Add rows as necessary*

Date	Action	Objective(s)	Observations/Notes (chemicals, equipment used, and special issues)

Table 3: Seed Mix. *Seed mix labels, if available, may be attached. List the species included in the seed mix in Table 3. Include any special notes here regarding why the species were chosen.*

Species	Percent	Seeds/ft^2	Pure Live Seeds (lb/acre)

Table 4: Planting.

Date	
Methods(s) and Planting Equipment	
Planting Depths	
Seeding Rate (lb per acre or seeds per foot)	
Special Actions Taken	
Fertilizers/Soil Amendments	

Table 5: Postplanting Actions and Observations. *Summarize specific measures taken, why they were taken, and any observations regarding their success. Also, include inspections, monitoring, and observations of events that could affect project outcomes like extreme weather or wildfires. Add rows as necessary.*

Date	Action	Observations/Notes (weed control chemicals and equipment used, effectiveness, inspection observations, any special issues)

Attachments

Site map: *Provide a map or aerial image delineating the restoration site. The following website is a useful tool for producing site maps and getting detailed soils information:* **http://websoilsurvey.nrcs.usda.gov/app/WebSoilSurvey. aspx.** *Site-specific information on soil types, together with an aerial image, can be obtained using the "Area of Interest" tab to delineate the site. The "Soil Map" tab will show the soil types, together with descriptions of each. You may be able to download all this information in a custom soils report using the "Shopping Cart" feature, depending on your operating system. Mozilla Firefox seems to work better than Internet Explorer. You will need to disable popup blockers to download information (see "Frequently Asked Questions" and "Known Problems" under the "Help" tab). Natural Resources Conservation Service offices can also provide soil maps.*

Google Earth is another useful tool for delineating site locations on aerial imagery and obtaining precise elevations and adjacent land use information. Oftentimes, this site has imagery from multiple dates, which can be useful for getting a historic perspective.

Preproject images: *Include preproject photograph(s) and/or reference site photograph(s) as an attachment.*

Postproject images: *Include postproject photograph(s) as an attachment.*

Postproject characterization data: *Attach any monitoring data, if any, as an attachment.*

Appendix 3. Planning Form for Restoring Degraded Shrub-Steppe

I. Restoration Goals

Primary goal:
Secondary goal(s): *(if needed)*

II. Site Assessment

General description of starting state:

Physical Conditions	
Area	
Elevation	
Aspect	
Slope	
Annual Precipitation	
Major Soil Types (depth, texture, other features)	

Note where conditions deviate from the normal range of variability.

Biological Conditions	Dominant Species	% Cover
Shrubs		
Grasses		
Forbs		
Weeds		
Soil Crust Status		
Other Vegetation Notes		

Ecological Processes and Site History	
Fire History, Visible Effects	
Grazing History, Visible Effects	
Erosion	
Other Observations	

Landscape Context	
Adjacent Land Uses	
Extent and Condition of Adjacent Native Habitat	
Status of Nearby Weed Infestations	

Reference Site

Note site locations or sources of information (e.g., ecological site descriptions).

Species (add rows as necessary)	Cover

III. Restoration Objectives

General description of restored state:

As needed, include composition, distribution, and structure details and temporal and spatial specificity.

Short-term objectives:

1.

2.

3.

Longer term objectives:

1.

2.

3.

IV. Interventions Needed

General description of transition from starting to restored states:

As needed, describe changes required in species (abundance and distribution).

1. Weeds to be controlled:

2. Shrubs (reduction or enhancement):

3. Grasses:

4. Forbs:

5. Other changes needed to site (site conditions, disturbances, etc.):

V. Project Feasibility and Cost Assessment

Evaluation of availability of manpower, equipment, and seeds and assessment of cost versus available funds.

1. Manpower needs

Personnel *add as necessary*	In House	Rent/Contract
Tractor driver	X	
Aerial herbicide applicator		X

2. Equipment needs

Equipment *add as necessary*	In House	Rent/Contract
Tractor	X	
Tined harrow	X	
Truax seed drill	X	

3. Seed availability

Assess commercial availability of needed seed. If not available, can it be collected and propagated to supply needs?

Species *add as necessary*	Source	Quantity Available	Quantity Needed
Species x	ABC Native Seed	600 lb	20 lb
Species y	ABC Native Seed	10 lb	8 lb
Species z	ABC Native Seed	0	2 lb

4. General cost versus funding comparison

Do a first-cut cost assessment to evaluate overall project feasibility.

Year	1	2	3	4
Estimated Project Cost				
Assured (or likely) Funds				

VI. Identifying Restoration Treatments

Proceed through the decision tree to plan necessary actions. Populate the table with steps identified in the tree.

Restoration Steps	Proposed Treatments		
Reduce shrub density	Aerial application Imazapic @ 70 g/ha		
Reduce annual weeds	Late winter aerial application of Roundup @200 g/ha	Repeat if necessary	
Seed bunchgrasses and forbs	Aerial seed mix of 4 bunchgrasses	Drill seed 12-forb mix into 5 islands where sagebrush is sparse	Reseed if necessary
Monitor for weeds	Spot spray local cheatgrass infestations		

VII. Detailed Project Cost Assessment

Follow the examples (Tables 7, 8, and 9) in Section 6.7.7 to approximate costs of treatments identified in the previous step.

www.ingramcontent.com/pod-product-compliance
Lightning Source LLC
Chambersburg PA
CBHW052005280526
45793CB00005B/853